BEHAVIOURAL TECHNIQUES

BEHAVIOURAL TECHNIQUES
A Therapist's Manual

RICHARD STERN M.D., M.R.C.Psych., D.P.M.
Senior Lecturer, Institute of Psychiatry, London
Hon. Consultant Psychiatrist,
The Maudsley Hospital, Denmark Hill, London

1978

ACADEMIC PRESS
LONDON   NEW YORK   SAN FRANCISCO
A Subsidiary of Harcourt Brace Jovanovich, Publishers

ACADEMIC PRESS INC. (LONDON) LTD.
24/28 Oval Road
London NW1

United States Edition published by
ACADEMIC PRESS INC.
111 Fifth Avenue
New York, New York 10003

Library of Congress Catalog Card Number: 77-85110
ISBN 0-12-666850-7

*Filmset in Great Britain by
Northumberland Press Limited,
Gateshead, Tyne and Wear
Printed by
Fletcher and Son Limited,
Norwich*

‖ Preface

"We have read the literature reviews, the numerous articles, reprints and books but nowhere does it tell us how to treat patients by behaviour therapy." This plaintive comment from many of my students was the reason for writing this book, which has been largely derived from teaching seminars given to postgraduate students of psychiatry who have become interested in behaviour therapy, as well as from case histories of patients I have treated. Medical students, with some training in behavioural therapy, and also general practitioners, who traditionally have little knowledge of behavioural therapy, should find this manual a useful reference work in helping patients.

Finally, psychiatric nurses I have taught frequently expressed interest in behavioural therapy techniques; indeed, many psychiatric nurses are now encouraged to specialise in behavioural therapy, and they too should find the techniques and case histories described here to be relevant and helpful to them in their work.

Behaviour therapy has grown in the last twenty years from a few techniques – systematic desensitisation and aversion therapy – to a broadly based approach often far removed from the theories emanating from the isolated laboratories of experimental psychologists. The author has been actively engaged in teaching and research in this area in the last seven years, during which great strides in the improvement of techniques have been made. However those working on the problems of psychiatric patients in clinics and hospitals have often lagged behind in their knowledge of how the techniques have changed. What follows is an attempt to redress the balance.

This book is unashamedly about *techniques* of therapy – a subject which is unfashionable among psychiatrists. Indeed, there are those who would argue that only clinical psychologists, whose discipline has a background in learning theory, should be concerned with this topic. However, the climate of opinion is changing and more and more psychiatrists are feeling the need to acquire therapeutic skills. Most clinical psychologists acquire these skills, but this is not the case for those with a medical training and it is to the latter that this book is primarily addressed.

My own knowledge was acquired at the hands of experts from psychology *and* psychiatry: I could therefore judge where the gaps in communication occurred, and hopefully bridge them.

Numerous psychiatrists and psychologists have taught and influenced me, and in a sense played a part in fashioning this book. There are really too many to name, but Isaac Marks and Jack Rachman were two of the most important. Other people who provided useful ideas for the book were Michael Crowe, Maurice Lipsedge, John Cobb, Sue Grey, Bob MacDonald, Ian Falloon, Bob Lieberman, Kerry Mueller, Carol Lindermann, and of course the many students themselves too numerous to mention.

June 1977   *R.S.*

‖ **Foreword**

Behaviour therapy has shown remarkable advances during the past two decades and is one of the most rapidly developing fields of treatment in psychiatry. Starting with the early techniques of systematic desensitisation, aversion therapy, and operant conditioning, there has been a development of new techniques, applied to disorders which had been notoriously difficult to treat by previously available procedures including psychotherapy. Behaviour therapy is essentially practical and necessitates precise knowledge of the techniques which require to be carried out in order to achieve the best opportunities for therapeutic efficacy.

Dr Stern, in this book, presents practical and detailed guidance for intending behavioural therapists. The text is illustrated with clinical examples which make interesting, realistic and compelling reading. He also presents very useful summaries of the main points needing consideration when planning the application of the various behavioural techniques described, and also outlines the principles underlying the procedures. The book discusses the use of behaviour techniques in the treatment and management of a wide variety of symptoms and disorders.

It can be warmly recommended for those needing practical guidance in the effective application of behaviour therapy to relieve a wide range of disorders causing distress and disability.

July 1977   *Professor Linford Rees*
President, Royal College of Psychiatrists.

For Benjamin

‖ Contents

"To heal Psychic ailments that we have contracted through misfortune or faults of our own, the understanding avails nothing, reason little, time much, but resolute action everything."

[Goethe, 1926]

1
Introduction

The Indications for Behaviour Therapy

Obsessional rituals

Ann kept breaking off from her story to ask "do you think behaviour therapy can do anything, Doctor?" She was a 26 year old housewife who had had obsessional rituals since she was 10 years old. At the age of 21 she had received 1 year 8 months interpretative psychotherapy despite which the rituals had increased. Whenever she left the room she had to return 5 times to touch something in the room "to draw off the harm left behind." She also had to turn taps on and off up to ten times and each time she washed her hands had to repeat this activity eight times. Her whole day was so taken up with rituals and repetitions that she was unable to complete household chores, could never go shopping, nor go out to work.

While she was talking to me, Ann kept rubbing her lips with her fingers. When I asked her about this she told me that each finger represented a member of her family, and she felt compelled to rub her lips with each finger "in order to ward off harm from the family." When I asked her to try and stop this activity she did so, but became more anxious and needed my reassurance that no harm had come to the family. "I know that nothing has happened to them really, but I still have to do these things even though I realise how silly it is."

Agoraphobia

Mr C did not seem at all anxious in the outpatient clinic. However, this 52 year old man described panic attacks on public transport in which he felt nausea, had palpitations and thought he was going to die. After several of these attacks he had begun to avoid public transport unless his wife went with him. He needed to travel by bus and train to take up a new job but was about to turn down the job because clearly his wife could not go to work with him every day.

Specific phobia

"If there is any possibility of her meeting a dog she goes berserk and we can't do anything with her," explained the aunt of an 18 year old student teacher, and then continued "I wouldn't expect fear of dogs to be anything psychiatrists should bother with, but now things are so bad, she won't leave the house." Since childhood this young girl had avoided public parks and if she met a dog in the street would run home. The family always went to great lengths to protect her and someone always checked the garden at her home to make sure no dogs had strayed in before the patient went there. She was about to qualify as a teacher and leave home, and so they had been sent up to a hospital with a letter from their doctor asking if behaviour therapy could help.

Social phobia

During the entire interview with me David sat looking at the floor. When he entered the room he did not even look in my direction, but fastened his gaze somewhere under my desk. He told me that for the last 7 of his 27 years he had difficulty looking people in the eyes and this had prevented his forming relationships with anyone. "Because I can't look at people they think I'm odd so they avoid my company." He had a gauche self-conscious manner as he explained how he had gradually withdrawn from social contact with people altogether and now lived alone with his cat. At work he found contact with people such an anxious experience that he frequently changed jobs and was now unemployed.

What do all these cases have in common? They all have problems from which treatment goals can be derived. The patients could all agree with the therapist on what these goals might be. In addition they were motivated to lose their symptoms and had something to gain by so doing. By the time the reader completes this book he should understand how to set up treatment goals and treat such examples as these described. In these cases the problem behaviour could be measured. Self-recording provides a method of feedback to the patient of his own progress, and allows the therapist to assess change over time. It would not be enough however to ask the young lady with obsessional rituals how anxious she was if prevented from rubbing her lips with her fingers. The question was put this way "how anxious would you feel as measured on a scale where o equals no anxiety and 8 means that you are extremely panicky?" With a little practice it became easy for her to report her anxiety on this scale. All the examples given were of problem behaviour which could be observed, but often 'behavioural' approaches can be used to change internal imagery, feelings and attitudes which are impossible to observe directly and are difficult to measure. For these cases the term "cognitive behaviour therapy" has been coined. The plan of this book is to describe the easier techniques first, and eventually more difficult behavioural approaches such as those subsumed under 'cognitive behaviour therapy.' To this end the next chapter will describe the treatment of phobic disorders – a logical starting point for those wishing to embark on therapy. Those with a previous acquaintance of the development of behaviour therapy should turn directly to page 9. However, for those without this knowledge a brief historical background to the subject is given here.

History of Behaviour Therapy

A brief review of historical developments in behaviour therapy may throw light on the present confusion of terminology in the subject, which has arisen through development of similar ideas in different parts of the world. Pavlov in the Soviet Union and Thorndike in the United States provided a consistent body of scientific knowledge of animal learning based on observation and experiment. Pavlov developed the concepts of classical conditioning using the dog as his experimental animal, and was concerned primarily with automatic responses, e.g. salivation to meat powder which later became the conditioned response of salivation to the sound of a bell. In Pavlov's studies the animal was typically held in a harness and had few 'choices'; he could either respond to the stimulus by salivation, or by not salivating. Thorndike's experimental animal was the cat which was usually placed in a box from which it could extricate itself by pulling various strings or levers in a correct manner. Thorndike, and later Skinner, were responsible for the development of operant conditioning. In this procedure the animal makes a skeletal muscular response which produces a stimulus for which he may be rewarded. The animal can choose to respond or not respond and can also vary the rate of responding.

In the United States during the 1920's and 1930's, J. P. Watson, Rayner, Jones and Mowrer were developing a trend towards using learning principles in the treatment of neuroses, and in an educational setting. By 1940 Fantt, Liddell and Masserman were establishing a laboratory base for utilising Pavlovian concepts in American psychiatry.

The work of Shoben, Dollard and Miller, amongst others, set the stage for the development and rapid expansion of behaviour therapy in the 1950's and 1960's.

Over the last two years, three centres have been responsible for development of individual approaches and advancement of behaviour therapy. In the early 50's Wolpe and Lazarus in South Africa were responsible for the development of laboratory experimental ideas on cats into a treatment approach used in phobic disorders in humans: systematic desensitisation. Wolpe took over Sherrington's concepts of reciprocal inhibition, which Sherrington had developed to explain the neuro-physiology of flexion and extension of a joint (Wolpe, 1958). Sherrington stated that in a flexor muscle, e.g. the biceps, contracts then the corresponding extensor muscle (the tricep in this case) must be in-hibited from contracting at the same time. Wolpe thought that if a person was made to relax during gradual exposure to a fearful stimulus, he could not experience fear at the same time as being relaxed, because the fear would be 'reciprocally inhibited.' Wolpe and Lazarus took their ideas to the United States and systematic desensitisation is widely used there, probably through this influence.

The second centre was London where Marks, Gelder and Rachman at the Maudsley Hospital, were exploring the use of behaviour therapy techniques in a variety of phobic and sexual disorders. Around 1950, Eysenck and Shapiro were also working in London looking for appli-cations for laboratory-based learning principles to the psychiatric clinic. Gelder and Marks were responsible for developing scales for the rating of phobic disorders, so that even this early work could be quantified and the results assessed several years later. Specific phobias were found to respond well to systematic desensitisation, but agoraphobia responded less well. Gelder and Marks thought it important to compare systematic de-sensitisation with a traditional group psychotherapy approach (Gelder, Marks and Wolff, 1967) and were concerned with the theoretical similarities and differences between the two therapies (Marks and Gelder, 1966). Rachman and Marks were also developing the use of aversion therapy, which might be seen as most clearly having roots in classical conditioning therapy.

The third centre of importance in the 1950's was the U.S.A. where the work of Skinner influenced Foster, Lindsley, Azrin and others to focus attention on the effects or consequences of operant or 'voluntary' performances as the principal determinant of behaviour. Ayllon and Azrin (1968) used operant reinforcement principles to produce change in patients with chronic schizophrenia. They worked at fairly basic pieces of behaviour such as the teaching of socially acceptable eating manners to patients who would otherwise eat with their hands. Patients were given small plastic discs (or tokens) which they could exchange for desired articles (such as cigarettes) whenever they used a knife and fork for eating. In this way patients gradually began to use a knife and fork instead of eating with their hands. This technique became known as "token economy" and was later extended to change behaviour in children with mental retardation and early childhood autism, and also personality disorders and anorexia nervosa in adults.

Developments in the last decade have been so vast that an historical summary at this point in time is not possible. However, an analysis of trends may be attempted. In 1967 Stampfl introduced the term 'implosive therapy,' by which he meant bombarding the patient with verbal cues to increase his anxiety about a phobic situation or object (Stampfl and Levis, 1967). Stampfl also used cues which he thought might be of importance to the patient's unconscious. This idea of increasing anxiety to a maximum can be seen as a move away from the systematic desensitisation concept. The move continued with experimental investigations of 'flooding treatments' (Rachman, 1966, 1969; Stern and Marks, 1973a). Flooding was originally similar to implosion, except that the patient was exposed to the phobic situation or object in real life instead of fantasy. Later on the whole concept of anxiety *per se* being important in this type of treatment was challenged. Hence the term favoured more recently is "exposure." This implies the chief therapeutic procedure is teaching the patient to approach and become 'exposed' to the object he previously avoided and was afraid of. When carried out in real life, rather than in fantasy, this is termed "*in vivo* exposure" and may be carried out slowly or rapidly. When carried out slowly it may hardly produce any anxiety to the patient, but will be extremely time consuming. This 'slow exposure' is similar in many ways to Wolpe's "systematic desensitisation." "Rapid exposure" is another term for 'flooding' and the two expressions are often used interchangeably.

Summary of the Book

This book is entitled "Behavioural Techniques: a Therapist's Manual." We have traced the development of behavioural psychotherapy from ideas which sprang from work in the animal psychology laboratories in three separate continents. The book is about treatment of the neuroses using behavioural approaches. The term 'neurosis' has a long history and was first used in 1769 by Professor William Cullen. In its original conception the term meant "a general affection of the nervous system" and was one of four main subdivisions of diseases, the others being pyrexias, cachexias and local diseases. In the 19th century Freud described three main categories of neurosis: hysteria, obsessive-compulsive neurosis and anxiety neurosis. In the Glossary of Mental Disorders based on the International Statistical Classification of Diseases, Injuries and Causes of Death (General Register Office, 1965, 8th Revision) no precise definition of neurosis is given. However, the neuroses are subdivided into anxiety neurosis (300.0), hysterical neurosis (300.1), phobic neurosis (300.2), obsessive-compulsive neurosis (300.3), depressive neurosis (300.4), neurasthenia (300.5), depersonalisation syndrome (300.6), hypochondriacal neurosis (300.7) and other (300.8). This most recent classification is based on diagnostic concepts which would be acceptable to most, but not all, British psychiatrists. This textbook is concerned with treatment techniques and so it is not surprising that the above classification, based largely on epidemiological considerations, will not make an exact fit. On the whole behavioural techniques are appropriate for the following categories of neuroses: anxiety neurosis, phobic neurosis and obsessive-compulsive neurosis. Other indications will be mentioned in this book where appropriate, e.g. in the treatment of social skills deficit and depression.

The second chapter in this book will elaborate the use of rapid exposure (flooding) techniques for phobic neurosis. Arguably, phobias are the most easily treatable condition for a behavioural approach, so this is a logical starting point for the beginner. Also exposure techniques are becoming the most widely used approaches for the treatment of this condition.

The third chapter will describe slow exposure or systematic desensitisation used to treat phobic neurosis. For a few patients this technique still has to be used, as the phobic situation may be impossible to produce in real life (e.g. as in thunder phobia), or the patient may be too anxious or simply refuse a rapid approach.

In the fourth chapter, exposure and other methods used in the treatment of the obsessive-compulsive neurosis will be described. Great advances in the treatment of obsessional rituals in the last few years have opened up important avenues of treatment for patients who previously had no effective remedies. Obsessional ruminations may yield in some cases to some new "cognitive" treatment approaches that will be described.

Chapter 5 deals with the reduction of undesirable behaviour, and describes how aversion therapy is used as an adjunct to the treatments. Covert sensitisation, electric aversion therapy and self regulation are all illustrated.

Chapter 6 describes how positive new behaviour can be taught to patients who are deficient in such areas as social skills, and the techniques of role rehearsal, modelling and practice are illustrated. Chapter 7 elaborates the use of behavioural principles in carrying out marital therapy.

Finally, the part played by behavioural principles in the possible prevention of psychiatric illness will be discussed. Despite the newness of these approaches it holds great promise as teaching a patient how to prevent further attacks of illness in the future may turn out to be an economical treatment if it prevents the need for costly psychiatric consultations, or inpatient treatment.

2
Rapid Exposure (Flooding) for Phobic Disorders

The efficiency of flooding is now well established and evidence for this is adequately reported (Marks, 1975 and 1978). However, the method of carrying out this technique varies greatly at different centres. The patient is confronted with anxiety provoking cues either in imagination or in real life for long periods of time. It is usually best to proceed as rapidly as possible to real life confrontation.

Mr C described panic attacks on public transport in which he felt nausea, had palpitations and thought he was going to die. He went on to relate how, after several such attacks, he had started to avoid public transport unless his wife came along too. He needed to travel by bus and train to take up a new job but was about to turn down his job offer because his wife clearly could not go with him to work every day. For the last nine years he had to be accompanied by his wife each time he left home.

Treatment of Agoraphobia used to Illustrate Exposure

Making the behavioural formulation
First the presenting history was obtained as above. The background history was then gone into in a systematic way: the only relevant feature that merged was that he had been discharged from the Navy because of "anxiety neurosis." There was no history of psychiatric illness in the family, and he was happily married, with no other difficulty apart from the presenting one.

Next the target problems to be tackled in treatment were worked out. His main target was "to travel alone on public transport."

After this it was necessary to establish a working hypothesis for the origin and maintenance of his symptoms. The patient himself gave a clue to this:

"It started with slight attacks of panic on a bus which got better when I left the bus."

"After that I started avoiding buses so that I wouldn't get these unpleasant sensations."

"When I hadn't been on a bus alone for several weeks, I found it impossible to force myself onto one. As the months went by this became increasingly difficult."

The therapist replied:

"It seems that when you started to avoid these situations you had increasing difficulty entering the situations again. Perhaps you learnt that the uncomfortable feeling was always associated with being on public transport. You never gave yourself a chance after that to learn whether you could survive alone on public transport, as whenever the possibility of being alone arose you insisted that your wife come too.

The basis of your behaviour therapy will be to teach you that you can survive alone on buses and trains. Of course you will become anxious at first, but part of the treatment will be learning to deal with this anxiety. We know from work with patients like yourself that anxiety eventually decreases if the patient stays in the frightening situation. You may have to remain on a bus or train for up to 2 hours before your anxiety decreases but when you have done this it will make it easier next time to go out. In this way it will become increasingly easy with each journey and the process of avoiding public transport will be reversed."

Railway travel was easier than bus travel so it was thought best to start here, as success early on would reinforce him and provide motivation for continuation of treatment. Usually there is an optimum time to spend discussing treatment: if this is too short the wrong goals may be set up, but if too long the patient's anxiety mounts so that it becomes increasingly difficult to carry out the task. The therapist and patient set out to a nearby railway station and consulted the railway timetable there. There was a train leaving in a few minutes for a thirty minute journey to the first stop. The patient agreed to take this train if he was allowed to take the next train back to the 'base' station, and if the therapist agreed to meet him at the 'base' station. The patient's proposition was, in fact, a courageous one as he was not asking the therapist to accompany him on the train. He was congratulated heavily, and it was pointed out that he must expect to feel anxiety symptoms and these were described to him. On the other hand, he was told that the symptoms would not cause him any harm. With a determined expression on his face he entered the railway carriage alone.

On meeting him at the pre-arranged spot at the station the patient reported his experiences and feelings: The outward journey had been the worst, he had felt panicky several times but had remembered the therapist's instructions about this. It was with great relief that he ended the outward journey and his tension began to mount again as he waited thirty minutes for the return train. However, the return journey was much easier than the outward one, and now he felt quite at ease and pleased with his achievement.

Walking back to the hospital from the station his progress was discussed. He had decided to face the train journey on his own and he had coped with panic attacks without untoward effects. He had no panic attacks on the return journey, so it was easy for him to see the advantages of forcibly pushing himself into difficult situations which he had previously avoided.

At the **second session** the following week, we attempted to deal with his problem of bus travel. This was more difficult as he could not be persuaded to travel alone by bus. At first the patient baldly refused to go onto the bus unless the therapist sat next to him. The therapist suggested that the patient sit in a different seat at the other end of the bus. It was agreed that they were not to make contact except in an emergency, but the therapist would 'shadow' the patient and not leave him alone without prior arrangement. The patient agreed to take an hour's journey in this way, and then they both got off the bus and had a coffee together in a cafeteria to discuss the session so far:

Patient: "My stomach felt in a knot for about half the time. I really felt like jumping off the bus but felt I couldn't with you sitting behind."

Therapist: "You really did very well to cope with the anxiety. You have shown yourself that you can beat it and that the anxiety symptoms eventually decrease if you can bear the discomfort at first. If you had jumped off the bus imagine how you would feel now? Well done! Remember how last week you found the outward journey by train was worse than the return? I think you will find the same true for buses when you make the return journey to complete this week's treatment session."

For the **third session** the patient spent two hours alone on a bus and was able to cope with this despite being alone, and with less anxiety than on the second session. He was strongly praised for his achievement and told that, if he could repeat the exercise for the **fourth session**, this would consolidate improvement so far. This proved to be the case, so that no further treatment by the therapist was needed. He actually stated at follow-up interview one year later "the more you do it, the easier it becomes." He was coping well at work and his wife confirmed his improvement.

This illustration demonstrates the ease with which flooding *can* be carried out in a highly cooperative patient who is prepared to face the phobic situation when asked to do so. It demonstrates how instructions alone were sufficient to overcome part of the phobia – the avoidance of trains, but the therapist's presence was needed to overcome the most feared phobic situation.

Some complications of treatment

1. A more complex treatment is sometimes needed however:

Mrs D was a 53 year old housewife who avoided shops, crowded places, and all forms of public transport. The background history in her case revealed that the onset of these symptoms was related to the death of her father from coronary heart disease: the patient also had similar symptoms to those of her father – a tight feeling and discomfort in the upper part of the chest. These symptoms had been experienced when she was out of the house and she had always rushed home for fear that she herself might die.

The rationale for prevention of avoidance of the phobic situation was explained as for the previous patient. The main targets in therapy were: to go shopping alone, to visit a crowded supermarket and to travel by bus.

The treatment by rapid exposure *in vivo* was similar to the previous patient. In the **first session** the therapist took her to a large square near a shopping centre. She was encouraged to venture into nearby shops while the therapist remained in the square. She refused to go alone, however, and insisted that the therapist accompany her. In addition she made conversation continuously during the session and it became clear that this was her way of distracting herself from the anxiety of the situation, rather than facing up to it. In the discussion that followed this was pointed out to her, and then she was not allowed to talk during the **next session**.

Another problem that arose was that she seemed to deteriorate in between treatment sessions so that at the beginning of each session there was no advance on the start of the previous week's session. Apparently on returning home her husband was preventing her going out of the house as he misguidedly considered he was helping her in this way. He had thought that if he prevented her anxiety attacks by keeping her at home she would improve. Hence he continued to 'protect' her by doing the family shopping so that she never had to venture out.

The patient had not allowed her spouse to be interviewed before at the hospital but now it was insisted upon. The therapist explained the rationale of therapy to both of them, and obtained the husband's cooperation as a co-therapist: he was to take his wife to the shops and let her go inside alone while he waited outside. The importance of these 'homework' therapy sessions was emphasised as an essential part of treatment.

In all, seven hospital-based sessions of treatment were needed, but in the last two of these the patient went out alone on public transport and to shops, where she met the therapist at pre-arranged places. She made excellent progress after her husband's cooperation was obtained and no longer slipped back in between treatments.

2. The problem of severe panics during exposure *in vivo* requires special illustration:

Mr D was a 35 year old mathematics lecturer who had panic attacks when on public transport or driving his car, or when teaching in front of a class. During the panics he had palpitations, began to shake, and felt he would faint. The attacks caused him to avoid public transport, stop driving his car, and recently he had to give up work.

He was a happily married man with two children, and no past history of psychiatric illness. His mother had fears of going out and avoided buses. He described himself as a happy-go-lucky personality with many friends, and he was not anxious except during one of his panics.

During the **first session** of *in vivo* exposure to buses he had several short bursts of panic and grabbed the therapist's arm lightly. He also cried out "help, help" to the surprise of fellow passengers. The therapist told him: "Keep seated and eventually the panic attack will pass. Nothing terrible will happen to you. Whatever happens don't run off the bus now or you will find it very difficult in future to overcome this." Then, as the patient calmed down and looked reassured: "That was very good. I'm glad you did not run away during the panic attack. This shows you can cope if you try hard."

After this point in therapy the patient made rapid progress and after four sessions with the therapist accompanying him, he was able to travel to work alone and resume his lecturing.

A special interest of this case was that he still had panic attacks at three year follow-up but was not avoiding the phobic situations. The panic attacks were treated with oral diazepam, 5mg, given at the onset of an attack. This relieved the symptoms somewhat, but he was also heavily reassured that no untoward effects would follow from a panic attack: his main worry was that he might die of a heart attack during this time. Pointing out that he would not die may have been helpful too. He was also heavily encouraged not to run away and avoid the situation he found himself in during the panic attack.

The use of a sedative drug in this case for panic attacks was clearly helpful. In other cases it is uncertain whether giving diazepam in combination with exposure is helpful. In some cases rapid exposure is made possible if the patient takes a tablet first. This may be because of a psychological effect or a pharmacological one. In general it is probably best to avoid the use of drugs if possible as often the patient comes to behaviour therapy with a history of failure of tranquilliser or anti-depressant medication. The value of combining antidepressant medi-cation and behaviour therapy is currently under investigation.

Rapid exposure is useful in selected patients with phobic disorders including those in which free-floating anxiety is present. The patients must be well motivated and able to carry out what is required of them without using subtle mechanisms of escape. Contraindications are those patients with cardiac or severe respiratory disorders. As has been illustrated, the skill in carrying out exposure treatments lies in the clinical judgment of how fast to carry out the exposure, and a careful assessment of each patient's capabilities so that he is continually making progress which he finds rewarding, and yet is not so frightened as to be averted from further sessions of treatment.

The use of modelling

Modelling is a procedure often used to facilitate exposure therapy: in this technique the therapist models an activity that the patient is afraid to perform, and asks the patient then to follow suit (Bandura, 1970). This procedure was combined with exposure in the treatment of the agora-phobic cases mentioned, but is illustrated in a more obvious way in the treatment of a specific dog phobia.

The patient (mentioned in the introductory chapter) was an 18 year old student teacher who, since childhood, had avoided situations where she might come into contact with dogs. The family protected her in this way, and someone always had to check the garden at her home to ensure no dogs had strayed in before the patient went there. She had to cross the road to avoid dogs and never went into public parks for the same reason. An interesting point in her past history was that her mother remembered that at age 2 years the patient had been frightened by a large dog jumping onto her pram. However, the patient herself had no recollection of this event.

In the **first treatment session** the patient eventually agreed to remain in the same room as a small dog, if the dog was never closer to her than 12 feet, and then only if it remained on a lesh. The therapist sat down on a chair close to the dog, and petted and stroked it while talking to the patient. After about 20 minutes the patient approached the dog and was able to imitate the therapist's stroking action along the dog's back. In the first session she could not be persuaded to touch the head of the dog, and would not touch it at all unless the therapist kept it on a leash. On leaving the treatment room after this session the therapist returned to the waiting room with the patient. The patient's aunt who was waiting for her said "She will never agree to having a dog in the same room." The patient then related to her aunt what had transpired in the treatment session.

Subsequently four more sessions were required where the emphasis was on modelling to facilitate exposure to the dog: the therapist modelled touching the dog's head, even putting his hand in its mouth. Eventually the patient was able to follow suit, even when the dog was unleashed.

Part of the treatment involved "homework" exercises in which she had to visit a friend who had a large dog. By the end of treatment she could remain alone with the dog in the friend's room. At follow-up one year later she was able to visit public parks, and had no fears of encountering dogs off the leash.

Summary

(1) Rapid exposure *in vivo* is an effective treatment for phobic disorders.
(2) Realistic treatment targets must be decided at the outset to which the patient must agree.
(3) Patients must be given a rationale or framework for the method of treatment.
(4) The speed of exposure must be assessed for each patient.
(5) Patients must not be allowed subtle mechanisms of escape from the phobic situation.
(6) The patient's spouse should be informed of the aims of therapy and act as co-therapist.
(7) "Homework" practice in between treatment sessions is important.
(8) Modelling is a useful aid to facilitate exposure.

(9) The relative's idea of what a patient can carry out in treatment is not necessarily correct.

(10) Severe panic reactions during the treatment should not prevent success as long as these are managed correctly.

(11) The therapist's presence is not always necessary during the exposure sessions, but often *is* needed during exposure to the *most* feared phobic situation.

(12) Patients with cardiac or severe respiratory disorders are *not* suitable for rapid exposure techniques.

3
Slow Exposure (Desensitisation) for Phobic Disorders

The groundwork of the previous chapter showed how exposure techniques are used in the treatment of phobias. Unfortunately not all cases respond to the rapid approach, and so a more gradual, long drawn out treatment is needed. We have had examples of rapid exposure *in vivo* and examples will be given now where *in vivo* techniques are impossible, forcing the therapist to use an alternative. *Imaginal exposure*: Some patients need these images presented in a very gradual way, and also need *relaxation* exercises if they are to cope even with this. Such patients would then be receiving the treatment known as *systematic desensitisation*. Systematic desensitisation was the first important technique in behaviour therapy, and has been one of the most extensively evaluated behaviour therapy procedures. Over 500 experimental enquiries suggest that it is effective for helping phobic disorders, but recently serious doubt has been cast on the importance of relaxation in the procedure (Waters *et al.*, 1972; Benjamin *et al.*, 1972). These, and other studies, have suggested that the use of a hierarchy as originally described by Wolpe may often be redundant. Most textbooks carry a detailed account of how to construct a hierarchy and how to carry out the relaxation for systematic desensitisation (Wolpe, 1969). This is of mainly historical importance now as emphasised in Chapter 1. It is only used today in those patients for whom real life exposure is impracticable, e.g. thunder phobia, fear of taking examinations, or those cases where the patient refuses slow exposure technique on the grounds that it is too anxiety provoking.

This classification of exposure-type treatments along a continuum can be represented diagrammatically:

SPEED OF EXPOSURE

FAST   SLOW

Rapid exposure   ──────────────▶   Systematic
in vivo   desensitisation

For various reasons Mr G would not allow therapy to proceed at a fast pace. He was a 58 year old, professional man whose main problems were height phobia and agoraphobia. When he went out he carried a heavy bag which gave him confidence, or, in his own words: "I feel anchored to the ground by the bag and this helps me cope with the fear." He found it difficult to travel on underground trains or buses. In addition he could not visit crowded places, drive his car over a fly-over or climb stairs. The treatment targets were: using a stairway to the third floor, travelling by underground train, visiting any crowded place and driving over a fly-over.

Treatment of Height Phobia and Agoraphobia using Slow Exposure

Treatment began with exposure to the least threatening item: this was walking along small uncrowded side streets with the therapist. Even here progress was slow – as soon as they left the hospital gates the patient clung to some railings, started sweating profusely and was clearly anxious.

"I want to return to the hospital at once" he announced.

Therapist: "If you return now this will make it more difficult for you next time. Try taking some deep breaths and relaxing. In a while you will feel better and we will continue along the road a small way further."

By the **third session** spent with the therapist he was able to walk along small side roads without fear. This provided the impetus for the next step – his fear of heights.

The patient was taken to a stairway in the hospital grounds and the therapist modelled going up a few steps and asked the patient to follow him. This caused great unease but with gradual coaxing he eventually was able to do so, and over several sessions was able to climb the entire stairway.

The next stage was to tackle his fear of bridges. Patient and therapist went up some stairs leading to a bridge which crossed a busy road near an underground railway station. Suddenly the patient grabbed the therapist's arm, saying: "Help! I can't go on. I feel dizzy. I feel I'm going to die."

Passers-by in the street looked amazed and a small crowd gathered. The therapist replied: "Just sit down and the feeling of dizziness will pass. You won't die. Nothing terrible is going to happen. Just wait for the panic to pass – you know that it will go just as it has done in the past."

Eventually the crowd of onlookers dispersed, and the patient was able to overcome his anxiety. At the next session the therapist persisted gently with the targets and helped the patient get used to the bridge across the road with increasing success. The patient then agreed to go with the therapist on a foot-bridge across the River Thames, at first achieving not more than 10 yards onto the bridge.

Meanwhile, he cooperated increasingly in performing tasks set for him between sessions, and drove as instructed twice daily across a fly-over. He travelled by tube and train, and visited busy streets and shopping centres alone, as instructed by the therapist.

His fear of heights on the Thames bridge continued and the patient decided to treat this problem by himself at his own pace. The therapist agreed to this, sensing that the problem would require many hours of exposure, and instead helped with the target of crowded places. They had already visited shopping centres and now focused their efforts on lecture theatres. Initially the patient sat in an empty lecture theatre, first with the therapist, then alone. Thereafter he attended actual lectures, first in a seat from which he could escape easily, and then sitting at the front from where it would have been hardest to escape. He often feared he might disgrace himself by interrupting the lecturer but these panics eventually subsided and disappeared. On instructions from the therapist he then attended lectures related to his work in many institutions, including day-long conferences, and reported that he was almost completely at ease in them.

At this point the patient was reluctant to terminate treatment, and seemed to wish to keep the therapist's interest by raising phobias which still had to be dealt with. This problem was handled by gradually weaning the patient from therapy by monitoring progress over the telephone.

Treatment took place over 50 weeks, and consumed much therapist effort. It involved 39 therapist sessions, lasting 63 hours in all, of which 53 consisted of exposure of the patient to the real phobic situation in the presence of the therapist. The patient maintained his gains to the 12 month follow-up, and resumed all his former responsibilities. His wife reported marked improvement in their marital relationship. He travelled to Wales alone by train, and set himself other tasks to overcome his residual problem in travelling.

Mr G demonstrates how complex cases can be treated with slow exposure, even when it appears at the outset that the patient is unlikely to cooperate in treatment. Success at the first goal (walking beyond the gates of the hospital in the presence of the therapist) was highly praised and reinforced. In this way gradual step-wise progress could be achieved until confidence was gained in other areas.

Slow exposure is by definition time consuming both for patient and therapist, and for this reason alone it is often worth while attempting rapid exposure where practicable. Pacing exposure is a subtle matter, embodying all the therapist's skill and judgment. This skill is gradually acquired, often through trial and error.

Treatment of Agoraphobia with Involvement of Spouse in Therapy

Mr H seemed like a good case for rapid exposure. He had agoraphobic symptoms and the target problems were to travel alone by bus, and to visit shops alone. After **four sessions** of rapid *in vivo* exposure to these situations nothing much had been achieved. He telephoned the therapist to say that he would not attend again for treatment, but was persuaded to come along for an interview, together with his wife. She described how she had to follow her husband to work by day by driving behind him in her car. Unless she did this he was too anxious even to drive to work in his own car.

The emphasis was now switched to a more gradual approach. He began by just walking to the bus stop with the therapist and thinking about getting on the bus without actually doing so. After an hour of this procedure he entered a stationary bus in a bus station (with the cooperation of the bus company) and sat on the bus with the therapist for an hour. Next he repeated these two steps without the therapist. On close questioning it turned out that busy traffic conditions were most worrying for him, so the next attempt on a moving bus was performed in a pleasant country area which he found less threatening. The bus was not crowded and the therapist was reassuring and supportive, taking steps to allay any anxiety that he observed. Later a more crowded bus was attempted and this was repeated for three further sessions before moving on to bus travel in an urban area. After this the therapist gradually phased himself out of the sessions so that by the 15th session of *slow* exposure the patient could cope with bus travel without difficulty.

At the end of treatment he was also able to drive his car without his wife following behind, but steadfastly refused ever to venture into an underground train. In view of the fact that he never really needed to travel by underground train this was not a great disability. His main problem with travel was greatly helped by slow exposure, and he remained confident when travelling alone by bus and car at follow-up one year later.

Both cases described above involved exposure *in vivo* for agoraphobia. Treatment may be carried out even more slowly by preceding the *in vivo* sessions with imaginal exposure. There is some evidence that this may be useful (Johnson *et al.*, 1976) but in most cases *in vivo* procedures appear to be most effective where they are practicable. In some cases, however, it may not be possible to recreate the situation in real life.

Treatment of Thunder Phobia Illustrating Imaginal Technique

Joan would listen avidly to radio weather broadcasts and if there was any possibility of a thunderstorm, she installed herself in a cupboard under the stairs. She had been afraid of thunderstorms since childhood and her pattern of avoidance greatly incapacitated her life: she could not venture out to work many days a year, and her social life was greatly restricted. Any attempt at real life exposure was impracticable as the therapist could not be on hand at a moment's notice. When a tape recording of a thunderstorm was recorded and played back to the patient, she listened to it impassively and unmoved, stating afterwards "that was not the real thing – it did not affect me at all." This situation remained the same when professional quadraphonic sound amplification was used to play back a recording of a thunderstorm at maximum sound levels.

Systematic desensitisation commenced with muscle relaxation training, as described by Jacobsen (1938), but abbreviated so that it could be learnt in four sessions of about fifty minutes duration.

The technique of relaxation is described by Wolpe and Lazarus (1966) and begins in the following manner with relaxation of the arms:

"Settle back as comfortably as you can. Let yourself relax to the best of your ability. . . . Now, as you relax like that, clench your right fist first, just clench your fist tighter and tighter, and study the tension as you do so. Keep it clenched and feel the tension in your right fist, hand, forearm . . . and now, relax. . . . Let the fingers of your right hand become loose, and observe the contrast in your feelings. . . . Now, let yourself go and try to become more relaxed all over. . . . Once more, clench your right fist really tight . . . hold it, and notice the tension again. . . . Now let go, relax; your fingers straighten out, and you notice the difference once more. . . . Now repeat that with your left fist."

The same approach is used to relax the left fist, biceps and triceps muscles in a systematic way. After this, relaxation is concentrated on the face, neck, shoulders and upper back. Then it proceeds to the chest, stomach and lower back. Finally, the relaxation is induced in the patient's hips, thighs and calves, followed by complete body relaxation. The exact form of the words used is probably not important, but if required those of Jacobsen are reprinted in Wolpe and Lazarus (1966) and Marks (1969).

More important than the exact form of words used is the attention to the patient's responses. Some patients become paradoxically more tense when asked to relax! This may be because they find 'letting go' very difficult and it will be essential to establish confidence in the therapist first. Attention to detail is also important: the patient should be seated in a very comfortable arm chair in a sound shielded room, and the therapist should use a bland monotonous voice to facilitate relaxation.

The next step, after relaxation has been taught, is the construction of a hierarchy. A hierarchy can be defined as a graded list of stimuli incorporating different degrees of a defined feature that evokes anxiety. The actual hierarchy used for the patient under consideration was:

(1) Being indoors and noticing cloudy weather.
(2) Hearing the radio broadcast of "high pressure" front approaching.
(3) Hearing the radio broadcast of thunderstorms approaching.
(4) Hearing distant thunder when indoors.
(5) Hearing thunder close by when indoors.
(6) Hearing thunder directly overhead when indoors.
(7) Hearing thunder and seeing lightning flashes when indoors.
(8) Hearing thunder and seeing lightning flashes when in the garden.
(9) Hearing thunder and seeing lighning flashes when in the city.
(10) Hearing thunder and seeing lightning flashes when in the country.

We now proceed to the desensitisation stage which involves presenting the above scenes to the patient starting with the least anxiety provoking item from the hierarchy. Before Item 1 it is usual to present a perfectly 'neutral' scene to practise the procedure and increase the patient's confidence, e.g. "imagine you are sitting indoors in your living room, sitting in your favourite arm chair reading a newspaper." This scene is presented after relaxation has been achieved. The patient is asked to stop imagining the scene and to continue relaxing. He is then asked to report his subjective anxiety on an 0 to 8 scale where 0 indicates complete calm and 8 indicates extreme anxiety. If he reports 0 or 1 then the next stage is to repeat the procedure with Item 1 in the hierarchy. When the image is obtained, the therapist then relaxes the patient and instructs him to stop imagining the scene and to continue relaxing. The patient then reports the anxiety he experienced whilst he was imagining the scene – this will usually be increased a little from the base-line measure.

The scene from Item 1 is then repreated as before several times if necessary, until the patient reports very little anxiety whilst imagining it. Then one proceeds to the next item on the hierarchy and deals with this as before. Three or four presentations of a scene are usual, but often many more are necessary. The usual duration of a desensitisation session is 45 minutes – the fatigue of the patient and the endurance of the therapist often being limiting factors. The duration of exposure to each scene is usually 5–10 seconds and the interval between each scene may vary around 30 seconds. The number of desensitisation sessions required for the above patient was 20. but there is great individual variation here – some patients recovering in 15 but most requiring over 30 sessions.

The difficulties encountered in carrying out desensitisation are usually of three kinds: difficulties in relaxation, problems of hierarchy construction, or the patient who cannot induce adequate visual imagery. The difficulties in relaxation can often be overcome by the use of methohexitane induced relaxation (Friedman, 1966). Here, a 1% solution of methohexitane sodium (Brietal) is slowly injected intravenously to achieve relaxation and the patient reports when he feels calm. Should the patient actually fall asleep then the injection is stopped. As the drug is an ultra-short acting barbiturate, the patient soon awakes and the procedure continues. Propanedid is another drug which may be injected in the same way. Claims have been made that this is safer in practice.

The difficulties in hierarchy construction are often a result of inadequate history taking or lack of full information. This problem can often be overcome by interviewing the patient's relatives when factors important in maintaining anxiety often come to light. For instance, a patient may complain of difficulty going shopping and a hierarchy of desensitisation to agoraphobia may be elicited. On interviewing the spouse it may become clear that the real problem is facing people in shops, so that it then becomes apparent that social skills training would be more appropriate.

The patient who cannot produce visual imagery often presents a serious difficulty for this kind of approach and the treatment may have to be abandoned. A useful technique here is to concentrate on a variety of neutral scenes before the desensitisation is embarked upon. Usually, patients find most difficulty in visualising fearful scenes but may acquire the ability after much practice with neutral and pleasant imagery.

Summary

(1) Not all cases respond to rapid exposure and sometimes a gradual approach is needed.

(2) A continuum of treatments is proposed with rapid exposure at one end, and systematic desensitisation at the other. In actual clinical practice most cases require an approach that falls somewhere between the two.

(3) Severe panic attacks often dictate that the speed of exposure is slowed down.

(4) Pacing exposure is a subtle matter embodying all the therapist's skill and judgment.

(5) Sometimes the speed of exposure in an individual case is arrived at through trial and error.

(6) On the whole, exposure in imagination is reserved for those cases where exposure in real life is not practicable.

(7) Systematic desensitisation consists of construction of a hierarchy of feared situations, training in muscular relaxation and finally superimposition of each item from the hierarchy in a systematic way while the patient is relaxed.

(8) In clinical practice muscular relaxation is rarely used and hierarchies become abbreviated to suit each case, so that patients needing treatment at the extreme right hand end of the continuum (see diagram) are in the minority.

4
Exposure and other Techniques for Treatment of Obsessive-Compulsive Neurosis

Confusion was rampant in the literature on obsessive-compulsive neurosis until Lewis (1936) pointed out that a subjective internal feeling of resistance to obsessional thoughts was a necessary condition to diagnosis. Obsessional thoughts (or "obsessional ruminations") are intrusive ideas often of unpleasant or abhorrent content which are recognised by the patient as their own thoughts in their own mind. Obsessive thoughts may be the only manifestation of the neurosis, or the thoughts may lead to actions designated as "compulsive rituals".

Miss J's obsessive rumination was that she would pass on cancer to her family. To alleviate this possibility she began to wash excessively. In her own mind she connected spreading cancer with the fact that she had been told warts could be spread by touching someone who had a wart. Therefore she washed her hands 125 times a day, used three bars of soap a day, took 3 hours to shower, and washed her hair repeatedly for fear of contamination by a cancer-causing 'germ.' She realised that cancer could not be 'caught' in this way and tried to stop herself worrying about passing it on to her family. She thus resisted the thoughts, but gave way to the washing rituals because, in her own words: "I feel a great sense of relief when I've carried out a thorough wash to my own satisfaction."

Miss J was 'diagnosed' as suffering from obsessive-compulsive neurosis on the basis of these symptoms. Of course diagnosis can always be criticised as Lewis (1957) pointed out: "Psychiatric syndromes at present have only a provisional heuristic value. . . . It is therefore still convenient to speak of obsessional neurosis. The obsessional neurosis *qua* neurosis rests more on its occasional tendency to become stabilised and systematised than on its exhibiting a constant grouping of symptoms."

The Behavioural Formulation

For our present purposes the behavioural formulation is more relevant than the diagnosis. Here we are somewhat handicapped by having no good learning theory model of obsessional neurosis. There is little in the animal laboratory which even resembles the complexity of such symptoms shown by Miss J. A common assumption, however, is that rituals have a basis in anxiety reduction, and this was borne out here by the patient's words.

The first step in arriving at a formulation is to decide whether clearly defined rituals are present which are time consuming and cause significant distress or anxiety if *not* carried out. Miss J had a large number of such rituals. The full behavioural formulation of Miss J's problems went like this:

An irrational fear of spreading cancer has led her to avoiding physical contact with other people and to excessive washing. Washing serves to reduce anxiety, and so tends to reinforce continued washing. Exacerbating factors include contact with her parents as her greatest fear was of giving cancer to them. For this reason she refuses to prepare or cook meals for her parents. Relieving factors for her tension included the washing rituals themselves, and total avoidance of human contact but especially contact with parents.

From this formulation 3 target areas for treatment were derived:

(1) Preparing and cooking meals for her parents.
(2) Washing her hair without rituals.
(3) Pricking finger on site of a former wart and eating from the pricked and bleeding finger.

The rumination of passing on cancer to her family was clearly related to her washing rituals. Patients who just have ruminations and *not* rituals require a different approach to be described later. At this stage it was clear Miss J did not fall into that group, and so treatment of the rituals commenced.

Treatment of Compulsive Avoidance Rituals

In order to control environmental factors and carry out treatment effectively it was necessary for Miss J to be admitted to hospital, where the therapist began by asking her to limit herself to one bar of soap per day. She was also supervised during washing and not allowed to wash under a running tap: instead she was persuaded to use a plug in the sink. In this way the number of washes and the time they took was slowly decreased.

In addition, the therapist 'contaminated' Miss J with objects that she considered might be harmful, and persuaded her to touch them: this included most objects that large numbers of people might have touched, e.g. door knobs. Serendipitously there happened to be a nurse on the patient's ward who had had a mastectomy for cancer of the breast. With this nurse's consent the patient watched the therapist touch the mastectomy scar, and touch herself and surrounding objects. Then the patient did likewise after which she was told to desist from washing, and later she prepared meals and ate them with the therapist and nurse. As the patient's fear of contamination from cancer improved, she was also asked to limit the items in her checking sequences one by one, restricting herself to checking each item just once.

After 47 treatment sessions the patient returned to work, and only used one bar of soap every two weeks. When she had mild obsessive thoughts she confronted them as she had done during her treatment. Her marked improvement remained at one year follow-up and she was able to go abroad on holiday without the contamination fears which formerly made such a trip impossible. Shopping without her mother's presence became a normal activity, and at home she helped with preparation of meals which contamination fears had previously prevented her from doing.

At this point it would be useful to compare exposure treatment for obsessive-compulsive neurosis with the exposure treatments already described in previous chapters for phobic disorders. In both cases, selection of suitable patients is important: they must be well motivated and able to carry out what is required of them. Modelling was used to facilitate exposure in both cases, and careful judgment of just how fast to 'push' the patient was very important. It is important to obtain the patient's permission to move on to the next stage in exposure, and it is crucial that a good relationship exist between patient and therapist so that the former can be persuaded and guided into the next step, rather than being bullied or cajoled.

The case described is somewhat similar to a patient with a phobic disorder, especially as the avoidance of contamination by washing can be construed as similar to the avoidance of a phobic situation by 'running away' from it. Possibly self-monitoring and self-regulation play a greater part in the case of the treatment of obsessional rituals. The therapist often has to decide for the patient what a 'reasonable' amount of time is, when applied to common, everyday activities, e.g. washing one's hands before a meal, taking a bath or getting dressed in the mornings. In this way the therapist has to act as the 'standard measure' against which the patient has to oppose his abnormally time-consuming activities. Thus the patient gradually reduces the amount of time spent on rituals to the normal amount of time that an average person would spend on a particular activity.

In general, the problems of the obsessive-compulsive encroach upon his or her whole life, and so treatment has to be more intensive than for phobic disorders. As illustrated, inpatient treatment was necessary and 47 treatment sessions needed before the patient could return to work. Thus exposure treatment can be more time-consuming, and rather more difficult to carry out for obsessional than phobic problems. To show how therapy is carried out in various types of obsessional symptoms, illustrations will be given of some main kinds of rituals.

Treatment of Compulsive Checking Rituals

Mrs K was a compulsive checker and hoarder who involved her family heavily in these activities. She felt compelled to check bills, receipts, money, door locks, gas taps, electrical and car switches, and household rubbish prior to throwing it away. As a result of hoarding, she had 300 newspapers on a sideboard and one room of the house completely filled with undisposed rubbish. Washing her hands or clothing took at least four times longer than the average person. In the year prior to her referral, her rituals had seriously increased, sleep was reduced, her sexual and marital relationships deteriorated, and her eldest child began to show abnormal behaviour.

The two main target problems were "shopping without checking money or shopping list" and "disposing of rubbish without checking contents". These targets were rated 6 and 8 by the patient on a 0–8 scale, where 8 indicated maximum pathology. The first obsession occupied 1–2 hours per day and the second about one hour daily.

Involvement of patient's family
Because her husband had been involved in Mrs K's rituals a conjoint interview was arranged. Mr K agreed to cooperate in preventing several of his wife's obsessive rituals. The marital relationship presented further problem: Mrs K constantly belittled her husband while he teased his wife that his job was insecure. This increased her checking rituals. In early

marital interviews the couple's attention was drawn to this, and both made "contracts" to change in the manner outlined in Chapter 7.

Treatment of the checking rituals was carried out from hospital. Mrs K was taken by the therapist for shopping expeditions and not allowed to use a shopping list. The amount of change in her purse was altered so that she could not re-check it. At first she took a great deal of time choosing each purchase, and was very reluctant to let the therapist prevent her checking the change. Gradually she was able to purchase items with less hesitancy, and to adopt a more relaxed attitude to receiving change. Before her discharge from hospital the patient went home with the therapist, and further prevention of checking rituals was carried out in her car and at home. After Mrs K had driven the car, the therapist instructed her to stop and leave the car without checking, and in the knowledge that the therapist might alter some of the switches. Mrs K's need to check the car rapidly diminished. The same applied to her difficulties with letter writing; she was asked to write several letters without checking spelling and punctuation, and to post these immediately. Treatment continued after discharge with outpatient sessions, a home visit, and four additional conjoint marital interviews. During conjoint interviews the couple spoke more civilly to one another but there still remained problems at home. Husband and wife disagreed about the times they should go to bed and arrangements for going out one evening a week. This was also handled with contract marital therapy, as described in Chapter 7.

Despite these complications and the initial gloomy prognosis, the patient made remarkable improvement. By discharge she had improved to the point where she only made one check of car switches, dials on the stove, and the back door. The couple spoke more positively to one another and made decisions more democratically. At discharge the target problems were rated as 1 and 2 respectively, and neither obsession occupied more than 5 minutes per day.

This case shows how the target problems can be decided despite the confusion at first sight. Obsessional patients often present a range of symptomatology and the therapist may be puzzled about where to begin. As in this case, the aim is to commence with a simple item ("not checking the shopping list") until this was mastered. Then a more difficult item was tackled, until gradually fewer symptoms were present. The husband's involvement had to be dealt with at the appropriate point before progress could be made.

Treatment of Compulsive Cleaning Rituals

Mrs L spent so much time cleaning her house that she had no time left to play with her two children or engage in leisure pursuits. This was despite the fact that she was an intelligent woman with a degree in modern languages. She described feeling extremely anxious before carrying out the cleaning and was very tense during this activity. When she had cleaned the whole house to her satisfaction, she felt a sense of relief. Compulsive rituals often serve to reduce discomfort in this way, as demonstrated by Roper and Rachman (1976). Although she made a moderate effort herself to resist this excessive cleaning she considered it sensible to engage in the activity, despite the fact that the new wallpaper was worn away with excessive dusting, and all her house cleaning left no time for other pursuits. There was no avoidance of dirt *per se* in her case, as she could plunge her arms into a dustbin without anxiety. She did not mind spreading dust around her house as long as she was allowed to clean it up afterwards, and all her rituals were centred in the house.

Treatment of this patient clearly had to be carried out in the patient's own home as all her rituals occurred there. Several studies suggest that this is often necessary, e.g. Rachman *et al.* (1973). In view of the fact that her tension and anxiety decreased after the performance of a cleaning ritual, it was decided to set goals of limited cleaning with an agreed upon time before allowing her to complete the cleaning procedure, e.g. the therapist visited her home and watched her going through an elaborate window cleaning procedure in her kitchen. The therapist suggested that she did not clean half the kitchen window (which was conveniently divided into two sections) until his visit to the house next week. The patient baldly refused this at first, stating that she thought she would not be able to overcome the urge to clean the entire window. She said "once the cleaning gets going I just can't stop." The therapist decided to help with this in two ways: firstly he marked the window that was to be left uncleaned by attaching adhesive tape to the relevant panes, and furthermore said that if she felt the overwhelming desire to clean before his next visit she had to telephone him first "to ask permission." In this way the patient managed to leave half the window uncleaned for one week for which she was heavily praised by the therapist and by her husband. Subsequently, similar procedures were applied until she could leave the whole window, and also keep down her dusting activities elsewhere to reasonable limits.

During the home treatment sessions an enormous cupboard full of cleaning materials: detergents, polishes and cleansing fluids, was discovered. As part of the treatment the patient agreed not to replenish these stocks until there was only one container of each type left in the cupboard. Moreover she was to save the money that she would normally have spent in this manner, and spent it instead on buying something for herself, e.g. flowers or make-up.

Along with the cleaning rituals, this patient had an overwhelming urge to be meticulous about everything. For instance, in the bathroom a shelf of lotions, powders and tooth cleaning materials was always laid out in an orderly manner. The therapist modelled disorderliness for her by squeezing some toothpaste around the sink, leaving the cap off the tube, writing on the mirror with soap and rearranging the lotions. The patient had no problems following suit, but stated that she could not leave the bathroom like this for long after the therapist's depature. She was asked to leave as much "disorderliness" as possible for as long as possible until the therapist's next visit the following week. The only item she succeeded in leaving was the writing on the bathroom mirror: the rest was restored to its previous pristine state one hour after the therapist left the home. As before, this problem was tackled by breaking it down to small items, e.g. toothpaste cap to be left off. When she succeeded at this for one week another item was added until she became less meticulous and her cleaning activities came under control.

Treatment of Compulsive Slowness

One special type of obsessional problem is that of *compulsive slowness* (Rachman *et al.*, 1973). Here the difficulty is that the patient takes so long to perform normal actions, e.g. getting dressed, having a bath or shaving himself, that ordinary activities such as going to work are impossible. Treatment is based on a "time and motion" approach where each activity is timed in detail and targets set each day for the reduction of time spent on each activity, e.g. a man who spent one hour shaving every morning was treated by the therapist being present with a stop watch and encouraging him to speed up his movements. The time taken each day was plotted on a graph, which the patient kept at his bedside. He was heavily reinforced with praise each time he cut down shaving time by even a few minutes. A target "cut off point" was drawn on the graph after it was arbitrarily decided that 10 minutes was an average time to spend shaving. Eventually the patient reached this point, and then the time and motion approach was directed towards speeding up his dressing in the mornings. In this way he was able to spend less time on "grooming" activities, and was more easily able to get to work. Compulsive slowness is a rare condition and the treatment briefly described here is still largely experimental, unlike the treatment of compulsive rituals which rests on good clinical evidence.

Treatment of Obsessive Ruminations

This is another treatment area where the techniques are still at an experimental stage. Well designed controlled studies are lacking but several single cases have been reported where success has been achieved (Stern, 1970; Kumar and Wilkinson, 1971; Yamagami, 1971). Some patients seem to respond to treatment and at the present time we cannot predict which cases they will be. The two techniques currently in use for obsessional ruminations are "thought-stopping" and "satiation".

Thought stopping

A 27 year old man reports that he cannot stop worrying about every small action he has performed. For about 10 years he would worry in a ruminative way about such actions as turning off taps or the car ignition. He hardly ever went back to check these actions but simply ruminated persistently about whether he had performed them correctly. His symptoms had become more and more worrying over the years and recently he had been unable to give his full attention to anything, so that his performance at work deteriorated. He could not concentrate on any job in hand, because of his thoughts about trivial actions from which he could not rid his mind.

Treatment consisted of 15 sessions, each lasting 45 minutes, given three times weekly. The patient was asked to construct a list of his obsessional fears, and this was used as a basis for treatment, those least fear-provoking being dealt with first.

Relaxation formed the first part of each treatment session, the aim here being to enable the patient to concentrate on the subsequent cognitive task. When relaxation was achieved the patient was asked to imagine himself performing one of the actions that worried him, e.g. turning off taps. When he had turned off the tap "in fantasy" he was asked to 'worry' about this for 5–15 seconds, then report by raising his hand when he had visualised his obsessional fear. A sharp noise was made by the therapist (tapping on the desk) at this point and the patient told to shout "stop" simultaneously with the noise. It was explained to him that when he said "stop" the obsessional thought should disappear, and the thought always did so. This was practised with further items in the list of symptoms. Eventually the patient merely said "stop" to himself (subvocally) and the symptom was controlled. Trials were made in addition with reality situations, i.e. using real taps, until he was confident in the technique. Then he practised treatment outside the therapeutic environment, e.g. at work. He was also instructed to practice relaxation (to ensure that he did not lose the ability) at least once daily.

This patient became very competent at the thought-stopping technique, and was able to use this to control symptoms in his life situation. He found that he could cope with work more effectively. Finally he described how travelling to work one day he had an obsessional thought about his umbrella falling off the luggage rack; instead of replacing it several times, as he would have done before his treatment, he relaxed in his seat and 'stopped' the thought. Although he remained an obsessional personality, it was thought that his personality traits could be used to a more effective end.

The part played by relaxation in this case is unkown, but in general, relaxation on its own does not change obsessional symptoms in any way. Probably relaxation focuses the mind on the cognitive task of thinking the appropriate thought, and controlling it becomes easier. The relaxation *per se* is not the therapeutic ingredient as when given alone it is ineffective. Furthermore patients can be relaxed enough to concentrate on the cognitive task simply by five minutes of relaxation instructions, when sitting comfortably in a quiet room. After this, the patient is asked to 'bring on' the rumination, i.e. to bring to mind the ruminative thought which normally appears all too intrusively of its own accord outside the treatment situation.

The third stage is the interruption of the artificially induced rumination, and in the above example this was done by tapping loudly on the desk with a large plastic ruler. There are various other devices that could be tried in other cases: shouting "stop", snapping an elastic band on the wrist, or gripping a hair curler with sharp protrusions. It is important that the patient says "stop" out loud at the same time as the interrupting, mildly aversive stimulus. On subsequent trials the patient should receive less aversive interruptions, e.g. the therapist whispers "stop" only. The patient then says "stop" more and more quietly, until eventually he becomes skilled at controlling the rumination by saying "stop" to himself quietly and inaudibly to the observer. This subvocal self-command is then used to control his obsessional thoughts whenever they occur outside the treatment situation.

Thought stopping for obsessional ruminations may be *combined* with techniques where a patient has *both* avoidance of an object along with obsessional ruminations; Mrs P had avoided sharp objects since a girl of 13 years. Such objects included knitting needles, umbrellas, scissors, nails and broken glass. At the age of 24 years she married, and became preoccupied with a particular knife – a bread knife received as a wedding present. Unable to use this knife, she constantly thought about it and worried that it might hurt someone. She developed the idea that perhaps she wanted to harm her eyes with this knife. Later on this idea generalised to all sharp objects and her husband was forced to deal with these around the house. She gave up knitting and sewing and was considerably distressed by the symptom. At the age of 30 years Mrs P developed the obsessional preoccupation that she might injure the eyes of her son, as well as her own eyes. Eventually she became unable to stay alone in the house with her son for fear that she might give way to her impulse. Following this she avoided touching her son, and Mr P had to take over his care. She also avoided anywhere she might come into contact with knives: this included shops and restaurants.

The diagnosis was phobic avoidance of sharp objects with obsessional ruminations of injuring people's eyes. It was assumed that the avoidance of sharp objects was a learned habit that was maintained by inability to allow her anxiety to be extinguished whenever she saw a sharp object.

The **treatment** formulation was therefore in two parts:

(1) To teach non-avoidance of sharp objects by exposure to them for long durations.
(2) To deal with the obsessional ruminations by thought stopping.

The patient agreed to having a small piece of glass in her bedroom, even though this caused great anxiety at first. The following day her anxiety about this had been reduced significantly. Then she was asked to hold a large piece of glass for one hour. At the end of one hour her anxiety was again reduced. She was given 6 sessions in all of exposure to sharp objects in this way and there was a steady fall in the intensity of fear and also in the urge to put the object in her eye. The objects used included: knitting needles, drawing pins, scissors and razor blades. Finally, she was urged to hold a knife close to her eye. This produced a considerable reaction at first, which eventually reached a plateau and reduced to zero.

At this stage the patient had no problems handling sharp objects and could venture into places she had formerly avoided (restaurants and shops). However, she was still distressed by the urge to put a sharp object into her eyes or the eyes of her son. *Thought stopping* was directed at this problem:

She was asked to relax comfortably in a chair and to think the following thought:

"Imagine you are plunging a needle into the eye of your son."

This thought was then interrupted with a loud noise and she was asked to think instead:

"Imagine you are lying on a beach sunbathing in the sunshine"

The procedure was repeated about 12 times per session for 6 sessions, as detailed in the description of thought-stopping given above. A minor variant of thought stopping found useful here was the substitution of the ruminative thought with a pleasant image "lying on the beach sunbathing." At discharge Mrs P's ruminations were reduced both in frequency and intensity to a tolerable degree. In addition she was able to hold a sharp knife, touching the orbital socket without anxiety.

Satiation

When thought-stopping is ineffective it may be worth trying a technique with an entirely different emphasis: satiation. Here the aim is to teach the patient to face his abhorrent rumination and *think* about it for prolonged periods until the rumination abates. Theoretically this approach links up with exposure *in vivo* techniques, and the mechanism *may* involve similar factors such as extinction, habituation or adaptation.

Claire was an attractive 21 year old girl who found it difficult to talk about her rumination because of its embarrassing quality. Her preoccupation, present since the age of 17 years, was that she either had touched someone on the knee, *or* wanted to do so and had to prevent herself. She might be sitting next to a girl friend in the cinema and the thought would occur to her:

"Have I touched my friend's knee?"

She would then ruminate about this and worry that her friend might think she was a "sex maniac." When sitting next to a middle-aged man in the train she would get the idea:

"I must touch that man's knee."

She would not, in fact, give way to her impulse, but would be embarrassed by her thought and spend the rest of the day preoccupied with the rumination, and the connected idea that others might think she was a "sex maniac" because of this. It did not seem to matter whether the person she sat next to was male or female, nor was age or attractiveness relevant. As a result of her rumination she began to avoid social activities, and would not sit next to anyone if she could possibly avoid this.

Going into her background history, it emerged that at age 10 she had been molested by a man in the cinema. This involved the man touching her legs through her clothing. Claire was very alarmed by this and eventually left the cinema and reported the event to her parents. This left her feeling anxious and distressed, and may well have prepared the ground for the development of her rumination seven years later.

Treatment: Claire described the typical scene in which she would get her obsessional rumination, and this was used in the satiation therapy. She was asked to think about the obsessional idea for a 40 minute period and the therapist provided the cues to prompt this if the rumination ceased. The therapist began:

"Imagine you are sitting in a train between 2 business men on the way to work. You notice the man sitting on your right. He is wearing a smart suit and reading "The Times" newspaper. Suddenly you get an overwhelming desire to touch his knee. You reach out and put your hand on his knee, and feel the cloth of his suit covering the knee. You give his knee a small squeeze. Everybody in the train compartment sees you, but they pretend not to notice. They just go on reading their newspapers. You know they are thinking "she must be a sex maniac...."

Here the therapist paused and asked Claire to ruminate in silence. A prearranged signal was for her to raise a finger when the rumination ceased. Then the therapist would provide more cues in the form of a narrative as before.

It was clear that Claire found the therapy sessions difficult and was at first embarrassed. By the fifth session she was no longer embarrassed: on the contrary, she reported boredom at the end of 40 minutes rumination. This may well be the mechanism of action. If patients can be made to face an idea which they have avoided because of its abhorrent quality, then the affect previously associated with the idea becomes dissipated and nothing is left to maintain it. As well as the five sessions of satiation therapy, Claire was instructed to push herself into previously avoided social situations. Going to the cinema with a friend once a week was a specified 'homework' task and this may also have been an important part of the therapy.

The mechanism of these treatments for obsessional ruminations remains speculative. Ruminations are usually resisted by the patient, but in these techniques patients are asked deliberately to invoke the thoughts either for a prolonged period (satiation) or briefly before its artificial disruption (thought stopping). This reversal of the prevailing contingencies may be important. Rachman (1971) has suggested that obsessional ruminations could be seen as noxious stimuli to which patients fail to habituate, often because they are in a depressed or agitated state. He goes on to propose that the rumination produces a mood disturbance which then potentiates the effect of the rumination and a vicious spiral ensues in which the patient ends up more depressed. In addition patients may be reinforced for expressing a disturbing thought because other people give reassurance for this. Thought stopping and satiation do exactly the reverse, and this could explain their action.

Summary

(1) Obsessional thoughts (ruminations) must be distinguished from obsessional actions (compulsions or rituals), as each requires a separate treatment approach.

(2) It is assumed that for most patients rituals serve to reduce anxiety.

(3) Admission to hospital is often necessary for intensive treatment of compulsive rituals. Only in this way can the patient's total environment be controlled.

(4) There are many similarities between exposure therapy for treatment of compulsive rituals and for phobic disorders.

(5) The therapist has to be rather more active in treating compulsive rituals than phobic disorders, and has to impose socially acceptable standards of activity on the patient. Clearly motivation and full cooperation from patients are essential for success.

(6) Cooperation of patient's spouse and family is also essential, as is home treatment of the rituals at some stage.

(7) In complicated cases of compulsive rituals, the aim is to commence with a simple item until this is mastered.

(8) The common rituals suitable for exposure therapy are: washing, cleaning and checking rituals.

(9) Compulsive slowness is a rare problem requiring a separate approach.

(10) Obsessional ruminations are more difficult than compulsive rituals to treat but some patients respond to techniques of "satiation" or "thought-stopping."

5
Reduction of Undesired Behaviour

It is a myth propagandised by such works as "A Clockwork Orange" (Anthony Burgess, 1972) that behaviour therapy, especially aversion therapy, is a method of imposing new behaviour patterns on people against their wishes. In fact, the opposite is true, and change cannot be brought about without the patient's desire for this: "a philosophy that credits a person with potentialities for active alteration of his own behaviour is the very antithesis of a mechanistic picture of Man. The goal of behavioural methods is to train individuals to become better problem solvers and behaviour analysts: to help them become more independent of the environment" (Kanfer, 1976).

Aversion Therapy as Adjunct to Other Treatments

Aversion therapy is a treatment in which an unpleasant stimulus (such as a small electric shock or drug-induced sickness) is paired in time with behaviour that the patient wants to reduce. This treatment was one of the earliest developments in the field of behaviour therapy, but is now rarely used in its original form as less unpleasant, and more effective, variants have been developed. One of the best known forms of aversion therapy was the use of apomorphine or emetine in the treatment of alcoholism. Administration of apomorphine was associated with the drinking of alcohol until eventually the drinking of alcohol itself resulted in severe nausea. The links between this procedure with classical conditioning seemed apparent: apomorphine acted as an unconditioned stimulus for nausea and vomiting, and the drinking of alcohol was the conditioned stimulus. After an intial period of enthusiasm for this technique, a controlled trial failed to show a definite advantage of disulfiram (Antabuse) and group treatment (Wallerstein, 1957).

The use of apomorphine has given way to the use of mild electric shocks, usually delivered to the forearm by a small battery-operated shock-box. This is called "electric" or "faradic" aversion, and is claimed to be more effective as electric shocks can be repeated far more frequently and timed more accurately than the pharmacological procedures. Electric aversion has been used in the treatment of sexual disorders such as transvestism, fetishism and exhibitionism, as well as addictive disorders such as alcoholism and cigarette smoking. It has also claimed success in the treatment of obesity and various disorders of children such as self-injurious behaviour. This manual does not deal with treatment of specific behaviour disorders of children such as enuresis where the "bell and pad" is now a well established use of aversion therapy. The part played by aversive techniques in behaviour therapy of the adult neuroses is invariably as an adjunct to the total therapy package.

Mr V explained to the judge in court about his urge to touch young women. His difficulties began at the age of 17 years when he followed a young girl in the street, and put his hand up her skirt to touch her on the genital area. The girl reacted in a startled manner and the patient walked away. In the same year he repeated his behaviour with another girl, but this time was arrested and put on two years probation by the Court. During the next two years Mr V made do with just "brushing" closely past girls and lightly touching them outside their clothes. However he subsequently gave in to his impulse to touch a woman on the genital area, and had to appear before the Court again. In all he estimated he had touched girls' genital areas without their permission about 20 times, and half the time he had an erection whilst doing so, although he has never exhibited himself. Usually he would masturbate as soon as possible after the act, whilst recreating it in fantasy. The most favoured subject would be a young, attractive blonde woman between 15–35 years who would be wearing tight clothes, and preferably a short skirt.

This presenting problem should be seen in the context of Mr V's life-long relationships with the opposite sex. On the one occasion he made a 'date' with a girl he was very anxious, and could not initiate or maintain conversation with the girl. In summary, the behavioural formulation identified two main problem areas:

(1) Deviant sexual behaviour consisting of indecent advances to women in public places.
(2) A deficit of social skills especially in relation to women.

Covert Sensitisation

Treatment of the main problem began with 10 sessions of *covert sensitisation* (Cautela, 1966). The deviant fantasy was: "a 16 year old schoolgirl standing in a shop wearing a red blazer, short grey skirt and dark stockings. He walks close to her and lightly touches her on the legs. He follows the girl out of the shop and along the street. He thrusts his hand up her skirt and touches her panties over the genital area, and holds his hand there for several seconds."

After obtaining this image he was asked to switch to the following *aversive fantasy*:

"A policeman is standing in a court room reading charges out. Everyone in the court is listening. Two newspaper reporters are noting down the details which will appear in the local newspaper. Everyone will find out about him. He feels guilty and sick."

To facilitate switching from the deviant to the aversive fantansy, the patient stung himself with an elastic band on the wrist. This provided a mild, but discrete, aversive stimulus.

After this session the patient was instructed to wear the elastic band on his wrist at all times and to flick it if he saw a girl that gave him the urge to touch. The following day he almost touched a girl in a supermarket and 'forgot' to use the elastic band as instructed.

A further session of covert sensitisation was given using the following *deviant fantasy*:

"He sees some schoolgirls wearing short skirts. They stop at a side road and wait to cross the road. He gets very sexually aroused as he approaches the girls from behind. He walks up to one girl and plunges his hand up her skirt and touches her buttocks."

The patient stung himself with the elastic band and switched to the *aversive fantasy*:

"My mother is standing in the kitchen vomiting all over herself."

The next session involved social skills training to social situations involving meeting women, along the lines described in Chapter 6.

Electric aversion therapy

At this stage the patient reported that he had followed a woman to a railway station, and touched her outside her clothes. She was not alarmed and just walked away. The patient was not able to use his elastic band as instructed, and so it was decided to use *electric aversion therapy*.

The deviant fantasies were as described above. After obtaining the fantasy he received the unpleasant stimulus (shock). This procedure was repeated 30 times in the course of one session lasting one hour. During the session the patient was seated facing away from the therapist with 2 metal electrodes strapped approximately 3 cm apart on his forearm. A commercially available aversion therapy unit manufactured by N. H. Eastwood and Son Ltd (England) was used. The strength of the shock was determined by setting it at a low level first, and gradually increasing this until the patient described the pain as unpleasant but not intolerable. This level of shock was used during treatment trials with minor variations in the level to prevent habituation.

Eight sessions of electrical aversion were given in this way, but social skills training was given also so that alternative new behaviour could develop at the same time as the undesired behaviour was reduced. In addition, he was given *escape training* which was carried out in the real life situation. Along with the therapist, the patient visited a large railway station in London. The patient selected attractive girls that he would like to touch. He walked up to the girl of his choice, followed a short distance until he became sexually aroused, then snapped his elastic band to sting himself. He then said to himself "this is dangerous, I must walk away" and immediately turned around and walked away in the opposite direction.

The social skills training dealt with the following problems:

(1) Asking a girl to dance.
(2) Coping with refusal.
(3) Dancing to a fast record.
(4) Dancing to a slow record.
(5) Being introduced to a group of new people.
(6) Shaking hands with someone after an introduction.

On being discharged from treatment he acquired a girlfriend whom he successfully 'dated' three times. This was his first regular dating experience and clearly represented a great achievement. At follow-up he continued to wear his elastic band, and needed to give himself an aversive stimulus on one occasion when he had been tempted to indulge his deviant behaviour.

Mr V's case shows the typical way aversion therapy is used in conjunction with other procedures, and exemplifies the use of electric aversion only *after* covert sensitisation alone did not produce the desired result. In all, 8 hours aversion therapy was given, but in addition he received 5 hours covert sensitisation, 5 hours of social skills training, and 1 hour of escape training.

Wherever possible the onus for control of unwanted behaviour is put on the patient. Mr W allowed this to a much greater extent than Mr V: he had a strong desire to be touched or masturbated by young children, and had carried this out several times. The problem had been with him for 17 years and he had served a term in prison because of it. Life had recently taken a new turn for Mr W since his engagement to marry. His fiancée was understanding and actively encouraged him to attend for treatment.

Treatment by covert sensitisation was begun. The principle was for the patient to learn to interrupt his old pattern of behaviour by breaking one link in the chain of stimuli leading to the undesired response. In the first session he described the typical situation where the problem arose: whenever he went into a public park he was drawn to young children playing there and would spend hours gazing at them, and planning ways of enticing a child to accompany him. He was instructed that whenever this happened he was to sting himself on the wrist with an elastic band, and at the same time think of the following image:

"A policeman is approaching you and asks you to accompany him to the police station. You have to appear in court and your name and photograph appear in the newspaper. All your friends shun you and your fiancée. In the end your fiancée is forced to leave you and you will never see her again."

This was repeated several times in each treatment session, after which he was instructed to visit a public park with his fiancée. He was told to look closely at children playing, and when he obtained an impulse to approach them he was to sting himself with the elastic band, think of the scene practised with the therapist, and walk rapidly away. His fiancée acted as a competent co-therapist who ensured he carried out these instructions, and then praised him afterwards.

After 3 sessions with the therapist, followed by 3 practice sessions with his fiancée he lost the urge to approach young children, and remained free of them at follow-up one year later. Clearly Mr W's fiancée was the key to successful therapy, as she not only provided the motivation for change but also supervised his self-regulation.

Another key to successful therapy with covert sensitisation may be that the patient feels strong negative emotion connected with the aversive scene. Mr Y was in trouble at the school where he worked as a teacher, because there had been a series of complaints about his violence to pupils. On each occasion his action was precipitated when he saw a pupil being violent to another pupil. When this happened Mr Y would impulsively strike out at the offending student with such force that the student often required medical attention. This aside, he was a good teacher who enjoyed his work. After the most recent incident he was suspended from work by the headmaster and referred for specialist treatment at hospital.

The formulation was that the stimulus 'one pupil hitting another' led to a response 'strike the striker' and he was unaware of any intervening thought, as his response was so rapid.

In **treatment** he first fantasised the typical event leading up to his violence. Then he was asked to switch his thoughts to the following aversive scene:

"You have been asked to see the Headmaster in his study. He says to you 'We have had another complaint about your violence to our pupils, Mr Y; I can't allow this to continue and I shall have to ask you to resign your post. I shall, of course, be unable to provide a reference in view of the circumstances."

When he visualised this scene it produced a strong emotional reaction in the patient. He went red, felt nauseous and looked as if he was choking. The reaction was so strong, that on the first occasion the therapist had to ask Mr Y if he felt well enough to continue. He continued for 5 sessions along these lines, and the strong emotional response may have been responsible for the success of therapy. He returned to teaching, and whenever he was faced with a situation likely to produce a violent reaction there was no difficulty "switching on" the aversive thought instead.

Aversion therapy techniques, because of their unpleasant nature, may have been responsible for creating the impression that behaviour therapy is a punitive approach to treatment. Certainly moral and ethical issues are raised by these treatments. An unpleasant treatment can only be justified if the condition itself is serious enough to warrant it. A case in point is the Lesch-Nyhan syndrome in which children show aggressive, self-injurious behaviour. This is associated with mental retardation, choreoathetosis, hyperuricaemia and complete deficiency of the activity of the enzyme hypoxanthine quanine phosphoribosyl transferase. In this disorder, repetitive biting of the mouth, lips, tongue and fingers develops early in life (i.e. by the age of 2 years) and rapidly produces severe tissue loss. It appears that the self-injurious behaviour is involuntary and unpredictable, but can be brought under control using aversion therapy. Clearly the use of aversion to prevent serious physical harm occurring in these children can be justified.

Rachman and Teasdale (1969) address themselves to the problem of chemical versus electrical aversion, pointing out that chemical aversion has disadvantages: it is difficult to control the timing of CS and UCR and there is confusion about identifying the UCR (is it nausea or vomiting?). There is considerable individual variation in reaction to emetic drugs and the duration of drug effects limits the number of trials which can be given, and also makes outpatient treatment difficult. These difficulties have been bypassed to some extent by the use of an odiferous substance such as asafetida (Wolpe, 1969) or a variety of such substances which the patient breathes through an oxygen mask adapted for the purpose (Foreyt and Kennedy, 1971). In this last study using obese subjects there was a difference in response between treatment and control groups, but this was not maintained at follow-up. Maletzky (1973) has used valeric acid as the odiferous substance in conjunction with verbal suggestion of nausea and vomiting. This procedure is reported to have helped one obese patient and one homosexual.

In the treatment of homosexuality, early work claimed great success for aversion therapy (Feldman, 1973). But it is interesting to note that the most important predictor of success in that study had prior heterosexual experience. Of these patients with prior heterosexual experience 80% improved whilst only 20% with no prior heterosexual experience improved. Bancroft (1970) divided homosexuals who had received *either* systematic desensitisation to heterosexual themes *or* aversion therapy directed at homosexual responsiveness into two groups depending on their overall improvement at follow-up. Decreases in homosexual arousal and attitude during treatment occurred equally in both improved and unimproved groups. Although the overall percentage of success was not high, the implication is that when success is achieved, increasing *heterosexual responsiveness by whatever technique* is a more important factor in treatment than decreasing homosexual responsiveness. One of the ways of increasing heterosexual responsiveness in homosexuality is by improving social skills. This is described in Chapter 6.

We might speculate why it is that behaviour therapy of homosexuals has been so committed to the use of aversion therapy. Wilson and Davidson (1969) argue that homosexual behaviour has been viewed by client, therapist and socially alike as "undesirable at best, and pathological at worst, something which should be eliminated irrespective of heterosexual development."

These authors also point out that the major promoters of aversion therapy, e.g. Feldman and MacCulloch, do not treat each case as an individual problem and they omit a full behavioural formulation. A more logical approach would be based on a detailed behavioural formulation which would emphasise the development of new behaviours by the use of modelling, behavioural rehearsal and social skills training.

The social learning approach as an alternative to aversion therapy for homosexuality equates neither 'normality' with heterosexuality, nor homosexuality with 'abnormality'. Along with other forms of less frequent sexual behaviour, homosexuality is assumed to be acquired, maintained and modified in the same manner as heterosexual behaviour. In this way we can avoid the value judgments of what is 'normal' or 'abnormal' behaviour.

Summary

(1) Aversion therapy can only change behaviour that the patient himself wants to reduce.

(2) When aversive techniques are used, this is as a small part of the total therapy package.

(3) In the technique of covert sensitisation the patient is taught to imagine an unpleasant scene (the aversive fantasy) which is paired with his 'deviant' fantasy.

(4) Electric aversion therapy may succeed in some cases where covert sensitisation fails.

(5) "Self aversion" in which the patient snaps an elastic band on his wrist may be used to interrupt an established pattern of behaviour, either alone or as an adjunct to covert sensitisation.

(6) Covert sensitisation is more likely to succeed when the patient feels a strong emotional response to the aversive scene.

(7) On the whole the giving of electric aversion therapy should be avoided, but there may still be a place for this in a few cases where covert sensitisation fails.

(8) The use of aversion therapy in the past to treat homosexuality has been misguided, and it is dubious whether 'treatment' is required except for those patients who complain of extreme shyness with the opposite sex. These may be helped with improvement of social skills.

6
Social Skills Training and the Development of New Behaviour, Role Rehearsal, Modelling and Practice Illustrated

David would not look directly at me when giving the details of his problem. He was 27 years old and had always been shy and nervous in company. He even felt embarrassed when looking directly into the eyes of a news caster on television. As looking at people made him anxious he avoided them. When other people saw him averting his gaze in this way – he would look under a table or into a corner of the room – they tended to avoid him. Gradually he had become a social isolate and now found he could not get a job because of this.

The target problem here was obvious: he needed to be able to look people directly in the eyes when talking to them. He was definitely handicapped by being unable to do this. He felt the greatest difficulty when talking to young girls or authority figures, and the device he used to cope was by avoiding any possible contact with these people.

Social skills training firstly consisted of *practice* with his target problem. Modelling was used to facilitate this: a co-therapist came into the room, said "hello" to the therapist and sat down. The patient watched this and was asked to do the same while the co-therapist sat in the room as observer. The ensuing conversation went like this:

Therapist: "What did you think of David's performance?"
Co-therapist: "First of all he did not look at you when he came into the room. Then he stood awkwardly instead of sitting down, and when he said "hello" I could hardly hear him."
Therapist: "Do you think you could look me directly in the eyes now, for practice?"
David: "No, but I'll try looking at the lower part of your face."
Co-therapist: "That's a great improvement, at least it's better than looking under the desk."

Then David repeated his performance and was able to make several improvements. These were highly praised by the therapists and remaining deficits were pointed out. The aim was to make positive suggestions to the patient rather than criticism. After this he practised again and was given feedback on his performance once more.

The co-therapist and therapist then modelled a 'normal' conversation in which ordinary social gestures such as hand shaking, hand waving and pointing were used. The patient at first sat with his hands behind his back and his eyes downcast. As he raised his head and used hand movements, this was reinforced with praise from the therapists.

After this emphasis on non-verbal expression – gaze, touch, appearance and gesture – the emphasis moved to *vocal* expression. Two therapists modelled the expression of tone, pitch, loudness, speed and clarity by the use of such expressions as "I beg your pardon, would you mind repeating that." It was shown that this statement could be made in a variety of ways, and the patient practised it until he achieved success.

Next *simple verbal* expression was modelled – the therapists modelled greeting each other as if they had just met in the street. The patient attempted to repeat this with one therapist, whilst the other acted as observer, and pointed out again any deficiency in the patient's performance.

In the next session, simple expression was tried out in a *realistic* setting. The therapist and patient visited a cafeteria and the patient ordered coffee for them both. He found it extremely difficult to look the female waitress in the eye, but eventually succeeded.

After this, the emphasis in treatment was on practising a more difficult situation of great relevance to the patient; going for a job interview. The patient participated in the role-playing as described above – the therapist acted the part of the job interviewer, then changed roles to demonstrate to the patient how he could behave more assertively. Finally, the patient practised the assertive behaviour when the therapist was the job interviewer. The patient was then set the homework task of going for a job interview for a hospital porter and to his great delight actually obtained the post.

We have seen how a patient who avoided eye contact was unable to perceive socially reinforcing cues. As a result of this, he was deficient in social skills and showed inappropriate behaviour. He could not elicit positive social reinforcement from others, and so had avoided situations where social reinforcement might have occurred. This was dealt with by teaching him eye contact and improved non-verbal behaviour.

Eventually more complex verbal expression and a realistic important and relevant task (going for a job interview) was acquired. Throughout treatment he was given 'homework' tasks to rehearse and consolidate the behaviour acquired in the previous session.

The amount of re-learning necessary to acquire new behaviour depends on the degree of disability. In the above case, ten sessions of two hours duration each were needed, but the same principles can produce swift and dramatic change where the area of difficulty is more circumscribed, such as the problem of fainting in social situations. The use of rapid exposure in real life and modelling, may be all that is needed as in the following illustration:

A 38 year old motor fitter with a history of fainting since the age of 16 fainted at his own wedding at the age of 22 and later on began to feel faint whenever he felt 'trapped in.' This happened especially when he thought he was the centre of attraction, and because of this he avoided crowds, theatres, and trains and always sat near the exit when travelling by bus. He was investigated for an organic cause of the fainting attacks, and simple vaso-vagal faints were diagnosed. The symptoms limited his social life and prevented promotion at work as there were situations he would not enter.

Treatment consisted of three sessions of about two hours duration each. Firstly, the therapist accompanied the patient to the hospital canteen where he was asked to remain even if he felt unwell. He was told "even if you should faint you are in the best hands as we will know exactly what to do to revive you." The patient replied "only women faint, I've never known a man who faints like I do." He was reassured by the therapist, who was male, that he himself had fainted during his initial days while learning anatomy as a medical student.

In the second session "modelling" procedures were employed in which the therapist demonstrated to the patient appropriate copying behaviours. He was shown how it was possible to put his head between his knees to prevent faintness, and that this action could be carried out even in a public place if the pretext of looking for something on the floor was employed. Later one co-therapist stood on a table in the cafeteria to attract attention and having done so, encouraged the patient to do likewise. The patient flushed and refused to do this himself. The therapist defended the patient's action saying laughingly, "no one in his right mind would want to stand on a table here." The patient subsequently recollected this experience as the key point in therapy: "After being so embarrassed when that chap was standing on the table and everyone was looking at us, I can never be embarrassed again.''

In the teaching of new behavioural skills social reinforcement, modelling and practice all play important roles. It has been said of social reinforcement; "Among all available reinforcing stimuli, the verbal and non-verbal responses of other persons are perhaps of greatest relevance for shaping human behaviour. Between one subtle smile or wink and the outright verbal statement of love or rejection, lies a large range of cues that shape, guide and control our behaviour in everyday interactions" (Kanfer and Phillips, 1970).

The use of modelling and practice is also thought to be very important in social skills training. When a patient has learned behaviour but his performance is inhibited by anxiety, the modelling is less potent, and may increase anxiety, particularly if the model appeared to be an *expert*. But where the model shows signs of anxiety but demonstrates *coping* behaviour *with* the situation, then modelling may reduce the performance anxiety of the observer (Meichenbaum, 1971a).

Treatment of a Disruptive Symptom (fire lighting)

The importance of practice has also been demonstrated: the key here is to start with a low demand situation where social difficulties are very severe: the patient practises simply shaking hands with a non-threatening therapist as a first step. He then moves on to more difficult situations: eye contact, simple verbal expression, and then more difficult tasks such as talking to a person of the opposite sex, ordering a coffee in a cafeteria and finally going for a job interview. Practice may be important for several different reasons. It may be seen as performance of a social behaviour which may be positively reinforced by others. It is also a performance that can be self-reinforced. The performance can be analysed with feedback from self and others, and can be repeated using alternative methods. Practice can be viewed as a 'game' that provides contact between patient and therapist. This raises the speculation that in normal childhood development of much early social learning occurs through the medium of games. On some occasions lack of social skills produces a disruptive symptom which can be helped by improving social skills. George was a socially isolated 26 year old man who had been before the courts because of a persistent urge to light fires (case taken from Falloon *et al.*, 1975). The idea behind his treatment was that if he could be taught *appropriate* social behaviour, the *inappropriate* behaviour (fire lighting) would not be needed. His target items were:

(1) Looking people in the eye when talking.
(2) Mixing in a group of people.
(3) Eating in public.
(4) Going to parties.
(5) Going for a job interview.

The similarities with David's case are apparent and treatment was along similar lines. Over a ten week period he was trained in the skills needed to perform his target activities using modelling, role-playing and practice in the real-life situations as described above. Self-monitoring played an important part in treatment and this served as a reward to the patient as he could observe his progress: each day he recorded the number of times he attempted any of his target behaviours. He also rated the difficulty of each behaviour. This enabled him to calculate the amount of stress he had tolerated in attempting to face up to his difficulties. Progress was reinforced by the therapist, but, more importantly, he was able to reinforce his own performance positively.

In the first few sessions he was also taught to improve his conversation ability, his posture and his perception of people in social situations. During the third week of training he was also able to eat meals in company and chat to nurses on the ward. From the 4th week he began to attend group sessions with other patients who had communication difficulties. In his individual sessions he was encouraged to express his ideas and feelings more confidently, and to this end was given a tape recorder so that he could practice talking about his feelings and playing the recording back to himself. In the 7th week treatment was focused on his personal appearance: he went shopping for clothes and learnt to avoid biting his fingernails. He began to attend social activities in the hospital setting, such as musical appreciation and discussions. At first he could only tolerate these activities for short periods but gradually learned to stay for the entire sessions. He was taught to dance in the Occupational Therapy Department, but found it impossible to dance at a hospital party. Despite this he was able to attend the party and coped with eating, drinking, and talking in a social situation. Treatment was complete after 10 weeks, and four months later he was managing to attend a government training centre and had completely lost any urge to set fires alight.

Anti-depression Skills Training

Mrs K presented with a longstanding depressive illness which had failed to respond to antidepressant medication. On interviewing the patient and her husband, it became clear that a major cause for her feeling of depression was the poor relationship with the patient's son and daughter-in-law. The patient felt rejected by her son since his marriage to a girl whom the patient felt despised her, and could not express her anger and resentment. She described a typical telephone conversation with her son after she had telephoned him to see if he had received a birthday card she had sent. The son telephoned saying

> "that card was rather silly – all those sentimental verses – why do you always choose cards like that, you know I don't like that sort of thing."

The patient's reaction was to cry and become more depressed. She and her husband were seen together, and the emphasis in **treatment** was on the role playing of alternative, new behaviours. For instance, the recent telephone conversation was role played, and the patient took the role of her son repeating his words

> "that card was rather silly – all those sentimental verses – why do you always choose cards like that" etc.

The therapist, acting the role of the patient, replied

> "I carefully chose that card for you, son, because I care for you a great deal, and I went to a large number of shops to select it and I think you ought to realise just how important my love for you is."

After this, the therapist took the son's role and the patient practised the new response herself. She was able to do this more easily after a little practice, and was *heavily* reinforced with praise by the therapist for her efforts.

At interview with her husband it also turned out that she became easily upset if he did not talk to her when she needed to discuss something with him. She would react by crying and giving up the attempt to communicate with him. She related how one day she needed to tell her husband about an outstanding bill that required payment. He was watching football on television at the time and replied rather curtly "don't trouble me with that, can't you see I'm busy."

This situation was role played with the therapist taking the role of the husband and replying

"would you mind waiting until the football match is over, then I promise to give you my full attention and we will sort out this worry of yours over the outstanding bill."

The husband practised this reply when the situation was role played once more, and the patient's spontaneous reply (without prompting from the therapist) was:

"fine dear, I'll get you a warm drink while you are watching the T.V. and then we will deal with the bill later."

In this way the patient learned that she cannot expect her husband's attention all the time, and he learned that she finds it annoying when he watches T.V. all the time and does not communicate with her properly as a result.

It also became clear that he had learned to pay her attention when she became upset and cried and this was pointed out. By doing this, he was reinforcing her crying and he was encouraged to be kind and attentive when she was *not* acting in this way instead.

The patient held herself in low esteem and when asked what she liked best about herself replied in a typically depressed way "there is nothing good about me, I'm all bad." The husband pointed out that she did have some good features – for instance, she was a good cook and "made specially nice apple pies." In order to improve her self-esteem she was instructed to say aloud

"I make very good apple pies – the best apple pies in London."

She actually laughed at herself when she had repeated this statement out loud, but with genuine feeling turned to the therapist and said

"Yes, my apple pies are pretty good now I come to think of it."

The next stage was to ask the patient to repeat the statement about her apple pies out loud five times. Then she repeated this in a whispered voice, and finally repeated the statement to herself (subvocally). She was given "homework" to practise this to herself along with the other more constructive and positive responses that had been learned in the session.

To summarise, firstly it was pointed out that certain factors were reinforcing the patient's depression, i.e. being comforted by her husband when she became upset after a telephone conversation with her son. The new ways of behaving in a difficult situation were rehearsed in which the patient pretended she was her son talking on the telephone (role reversal) and then she practised new ways of responding both to him, and her husband in the treatment sessions (role rehearsal) and in the real life situation (homework). The patient's husband learnt to praise her for more appropriate behaviour towards their son (reinforcement) and she practised saying things to herself that were aimed towards raising her self-esteem (positive self statements).

Treatment of Stuttering

A specific social skill that can be learnt is that of fluent speech in a patient who stutters. The imposition of some form of rhythm on speech for the treatment of stuttering has a long history and is reviewed by Fransella (1976). Brady (1971) described the use of a miniaturised electronic metronome which is worn behind the ear like the hearing aid it resembles. 90% of the patients who used this technique showed marked increase in fluency, but a large amount of therapist contact is needed in addition to the use of the metronome. Azrin and Nunn (1974) developed a more rapidly effective treatment based on viewing stuttering as a type of nervous habit which could be treated by "habit reversal."

It is a modification of the technique of Azrin and co-workers that will be described here.

Jo was a 26 year old clerk who had had a severe stutter for five years. When he spoke on the telephone he often could not get a single word out, and had lost one job because of this problem. The treatment consisted of two parts: firstly, the mechanical problem of his speech dysfluency, and secondly, his phobic problem – he was embarrassed in social situations and speech became impossible on these occasions.

Part one of the **treatment** took place during a single 3-hour long session in which he was taught regulated diaphragmatic breathing. He was shown how to protrude his abdomen gradually while exhaling, thus ensuring that he used diaphragmatic breathing. The therapist showed how this could be done by placing a hand on the abdomen while exhaling to check that the abdomen was being pushed out. The patient felt the therapist's abdomen in this way at first, and then carried out the procedure on himself. Next the patient was told to emit a simple sound while exhaling in this way, and finally he spoke a word, all the time keeping a hand on his abdomen to ensure that he was using diaphragmatic breathing. Then he was taught to start speaking immediately after taking a deep breath, to emphasise the initial part of a statement, and to speak for short durations. As his speech became more fluent he gradually increased the duration of speech. The instant he started to stutter his therapist would tell him to stop speaking, ask him to breathe out using the diaphragm, then slowly inhale using the diaphragmatic breathing method.

This procedure was first practised while reading, the number of words spoken per breath being progressively increased as he was able to speak more fluently. The patient read the first line of a book while interrupting and breathing after each word. On the next line he interrupted only after 2 words, and on the 3rd line after every third word, and so on until he was reading long phrases before pausing for breath.

At the end of this phase of treatment he was told how to practise overcoming the mechanical problem by homework exercises, and the emphasis in treatment with the therapist switched to dealing with the *social problem*. The patient entered a group of three others with stuttering difficulties and each patient practised speaking first to the therapist, then to the group. Then he had practice talking to a young lady, as talking to the opposite sex was specially difficult. A sympathetic hospital secretary helped out at this point! He then gave a talk to an audience of five people and achieved his goal of speaking fluently for 20 minutes. Similar techniques to those already described for teaching social skills were employed. Finally, he held a 10 minute telephone conversation, speaking fluently, and he was given instructions to telephone the therapist once weekly. During the treatment he was instructed to practise diaphragmatic breathing at home every day for 10 minutes. The total time spent with the therapist in this case was only 8 hours, and as most of this was carried out in a group this represents a most efficient treatment approach. At 6-month follow-up he was able to speak fluently on the telephone, and talk in front of an audience with no difficulty. In the study by Azrin and Nunn (1974) using this technique the treatment was exceptionally brief: one session of 2 hours duration plus several follow-up telephone calls. The benefit was substantial for all 14 patients treated and was as effective for patients who stuttered very severely (one thousand episodes per day) as well as for the patient who stuttered rarely. As with most behavioural techniques the method requires great motivation and effort to acquire the new manner of speaking and breathing.

Summary

(1) The target problem should be the most frequently occurring difficulty.
(2) The target problem should represent a definite handicap to the patient.
(3) The details of the target problem such as where and with whom the difficulty occurs are important to determine.
(4) The coping mechanism the patient already uses may have to be reversed, e.g. use of avoidance of gaze.
(5) Practice begins with less threatening situations, and works up to the most difficult.
(6) Feedback to the patient is essential. Here the emphasis is on what the patient did, how he felt, and how others saw him.
(7) Suggestions to the patient are better than criticism.
(8) Social skills training is a generic term used where new skills are taught in many different clinical situations, and many terms have been described in the literature, e.g.:

Assertive training (Wolpe and Lazarus, 1966),
Personal effectiveness (Liberman et al., 1975),
Anxiety management (Meichenbaum, 1971b),
Social skills training (Falloon et al., 1974),
Rehearsal and coaching (McFall and Twentyman, 1973).

(9) Social skills training can be used to deal with a socially unacceptable behaviour (e.g. fire lighting) by teaching appropriate social skills.
(10) Anti-depression skills training is a variant of social skills training which may be used where depression is due to inability to deal with a relative.
(11) Habit reversal is a specific technique that may be used for stuttering in social situations, thereby increasing fluency of speech and social ability. This treatment is in two parts:

(i) Treatment of the mechanical problem by teaching regulated breathing.
(ii) Treatment of the social problem by graduated social retraining.

7
Behavioural Marital Therapy

About 8 years ago Richard Stuart reported a striking phenomenon which was at first sight so glaringly obvious that it seemed hardly worth comment: the only way married couples will understand each other is for them to take notice of what the other person says and does. Stuart went on to suggest that the way to get the partner to change behaviour is for each to change his/her own behaviour first (Stuart, 1969). Also the way to initiate change was to *reward* the partner for carrying out whatever behaviour they liked in him/her.

"I want her to behave in a more feminine way" said Mr H at the outset of the first session of conjoint marital therapy. Mrs H was encouraged to take notice and respond to this, but the therapist pointed out how general this request was and asked Mr H to try and specify more exactly how he thought his wife could behave in a more feminine manner:

"She will not let me touch her breasts" he replied. Mrs H replied that her breasts were hypersensitive since the birth of her child, since when she had not allowed her husband to touch them. She agreed however that she would allow him to do so for a short period each time they made love, as she now realised how important this was to him.

The therapist then asked Mrs H what she would like her husband to do for her in return for this. She replied that most of all she would like him to put up some kitchen cupboards he had agreed to make but had 'forgotten' about for some time. It was made clear that putting up kitchen cupboards was a 'reward' for being allowed to fondle her breasts and the one activity was *contingent* on the other. This is an example of how positive, desired behaviours can be elicited. Of course a full history of their problems and background was taken in the usual way first.

Contract Marital Therapy
Illustrated in patients with obsessional rituals

Mrs H was 31 and her husband 11 years older. She had been disabled by checking rituals from the age of 19 years and this took the form of a compulsion to check switches and gas taps many times. Recently she had been unable to use the washing machine for fear she would rinse 'coloured' with 'white' clothing. She also became unable to wash herself because if she did this was accompanied by an obsessive idea that harm would come to her children. Gradually her activities became more restricted, until eventually she could do no housework at all, nor even wash or dress herself without her husband's help which was made most time-consuming by the rituals. In the last two years she became 'frozen' in the house, being scared to perform any action at all lest her children should become ill or die from an accident. If she did force herself to do anything, this would necessitate a magical 'undoing' of the activity by means of a phrase like "God forbid."

At 22 she married, and they had their first child the following year and their second two years later. Until then the marriage had been happy, but about this time the patient 'lost interest in sex.' The marriage then deteriorated, with increasing rows, rare sexual intercourse and intolerance by the husband of his wife's rituals. She felt he lacked understanding and sympathy, and both were worried about their two children being affected by the situation. Recently they had ceased talking to one another and he often hit her, causing bad bruises. They were considering separation.

The patient was first treated by daily group psychotherapy for four months with little effect. After this she was treated by prevention of the rituals at home for six weeks under the supervision of a psychologist – this was followed by partial improvement which, however, was not maintained. Her condition gradually deteriorated, and did not improve with subsequent treatment by 'flooding' in fantasy to the thought of harm befalling her children. Contract marital therapy was then begun, six months after the patient's first attendance.

Treatment of marital sexual problems
(Case taken from Stern and Marks, 1973b)

The patient and her husband were seen together for 10 hour-long sessions. At the outset each partner listed behaviours which were desired from the spouse. The husband wanted his wife to allow more frequent sexual intercourse, and to carry out more household work. The patient wanted her husband to converse seriously with her, and to complete household jobs that she had requested.

After each partner had specified the detailed changes wanted from the other, the therapist spent the rest of the first treatment session in pointing out that reversal of their non-communication depended on each partner asking the other for rewards. Reasonable goals were set up as alternative and more adaptive ways of behaving, such as the example given where she allowed him to fondle her breasts in return for him carrying out specified carpentry in the kitchen.

In the second session, a marked change was noted. The couple sat closer to each other and exchanged frequent smiles. They touched and praised one another in contrast to the first session. The husband announced that sexual intercourse had occurred daily since the first session a week earlier and his wife had enjoyed this more than she had done for many years. She had also been able to perform more housework than formerly. She smiled when relating how pleased she was with her husband's carpentry. Their conversation came to an abrupt halt when he remarked how inhibited she still was about sex. The wife looked shocked, blushed and remarked "It's disgusting and dirty to talk about that." She had difficulty in using the words "sex" and "breast" during the session, and agreed that she had all her life avoided talking or thinking about sex. To overcome this avoidance, her next contract was to read 15 pages daily of a sex manual which her husband had bought (Hegeler and Hegeler's "*An ABZ of Love*", and he agreed to decorate the kitchen if she did this. It was made clear to her that his work was contingent upon her reading the formerly abhorrent book about sex education. Subsequent sessions were spent in reviewing the behaviour that occurred between the sessions. When the wife stated that her husband had a habit of talking to her while doing something else, this was pointed out to him, and he contracted to spend a definite period (30 minutes) daily in conversation with her without reading the newspaper or other distraction. This was set up as a reward for the wife's efforts towards sexual intimacy. The husband then pointed out his wife's need for prolonged foreplay before she could attain orgasm. He could not discuss this with her, as she refused to talk about it. She was asked to agree to read the sex manual on the subject of foreplay and then discuss this with her husband before the next session. She managed to do this with her husband before the next session, and afterwards achieved regular orgasms. Most of her contracts requested her husband to perform carpentry or decorating in the home. Eventually her own contracts became related to her present disability – she agreed to wash and then

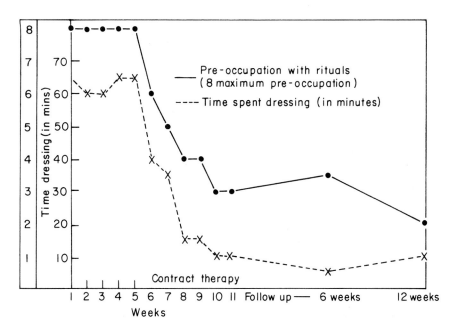

Fig. 1. Decreased activities of wife.

dress herself without her husband's aid. She admitted to lessened fear of doing the housework even though she continued to have ruminative thoughts (about harm befalling her children) with the same intensity. Her inhibitions about sex decreased as she continued to explore the new techniques described in the sex manual. Their increased physical interaction was paralleled by an improved emotional relationship.

There were six measures of progress in treatment: (1) severity of wife's rituals; (2) amount of housework wife performed; (3) husband's carpentry; (4) husband's conversation; (5) wife's time spent dressing and (6) frequency of sexual intercourse. The first four were rated on an 0–8 linear scale where 8 = maximum amount of the activity. In each case the spouse rated the partner on the relevant activity, e.g. husband rated wife on the severity of the rituals, 8 indicating the rituals were 'the worst they have ever been' and 0 indicating 'no rituals at all.' 'Time dressing' was rated by asking the husband how many minutes his wife took to dress unaided on the day of the rating. 'Sexual intercourse' referred to the weekly frequency and was rated by both partners together.

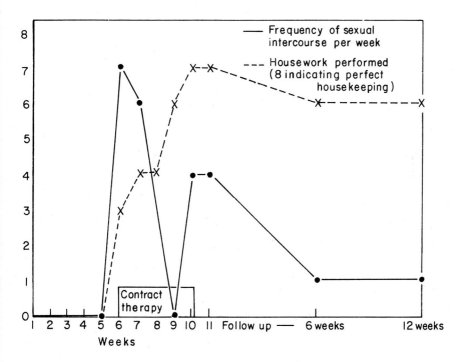

Fig. 2. Increased activities of wife.

Figs 1 and 2 show that shortly after contract treatment began the wife's rituals decreased and she wasted less time dressing while more acceptable behaviours (housework and intercourse) increased. Menses were at week 9. However, despite the decrease in rituals, the obsessive ruminations of harm befalling her children persisted. Rating of this symptom was not practicable, but while before treatment it had preceded rituals the ruminations now no longer led to rituals and to that extent became less troublesome. Figure 3 shows that the husband spent more time on household chores for his wife, and talked more to her, than before treatment. During treatment each partner began to relate more positively towards the other, and this found expression in both sexual and non-sexual ways. At 24 weeks follow-up the wife's improvement in rituals was still maintained, and the frequency of sexual intercourse was stabilised at once a week, despite some continuing minor conflicts.

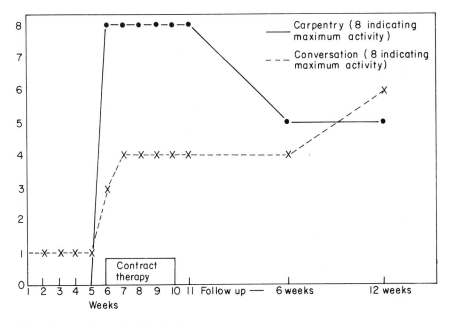

Fig. 3. Increased activities of husband.

It was important that behaviour identified for change was explicitly stated and from a defined repertoire, e.g. "build the kitchen cupboards" and not "make yourself more helpful", or "allow ten minutes fondling of your breasts daily" not "be more feminine." Clear, specific instructions are much easier to follow than general directives.

The couple were shown how to become mutually rewarding by the use of contract therapy. Over the years they had ceased being sources of satisfaction for one another or, in Liberman's terms (1970), had developed a "pattern of coercion." They were shown that each had to take the initiative in changing behaviour without waiting for the spouse to change first, and then they learnt the 'give-to-get' principle.

In this case, the improvement in sexual relations was startlingly rapid and coincided with a decrease in rituals, which continued even later when sexual relations became less frequent. Sex may have reinforced the resurrection of emotional ties, and reading books about sex may have helped by reducing ignorance in a sensitive area, as well as having an obvious desensitising function.

A common criticism of the kind of approach just described is that it is too 'simplistic' to hope to deal with the complexities of human relationships, or that it is an 'insult' to the intelligence of the couple involved. "Building kitchen cupboards" indeed *seems* a far cry from building up a good marital relationship, but this activity was clearly relevant and important for the couple described. Possibly the concentration upon seemingly simple items of behaviour is essential to the readjustment of life-long disruptive behaviour. Readjustment of behaviour may then lead to a change in the interpersonal relationship between the couple such that mutual understanding develops. On the other hand, it may become clear when the relationship defects have been unmasked, that separation or divorce is the best compromise. Divorce is one result of any kind of marital therapy, and the therapist has to accept this as a possibility at the outset.

In marital therapy the therapist is in a position to view the marital problems from the outside and can often see where one partner is deficient in his behaviour towards the other. The drawing up of "contracts" to redress the balance is one way of putting this right. It should not necessarily be thought of as simplistic: exploration of the reinforcers that each member of the dyad uses on the other may be an extremely complex process that requires great therapeutic skill, and also considerable self-observation and monitoring of behaviour on the part of the patient. The details of how to draw up contracts will be further described in the next case illustration.

Contract Therapy Illustrated in a Patient with Social Deficits in addition to Sexual Difficulties

Mr J was a schoolteacher who had serious difficulties coping with social situations. He could not go into the staff room at school, and was very anxious when meeting his head of department, visiting friends or relatives. In addition his marriage was a disaster: no sexual intercourse had occurred for the last three years and there were constant rows at home about household management, finance and the bringing up of children.

He had met his wife when he was 23 years old and she was four years younger. Neither had any sexual contact or experience before marriage. From the onset the patient remembered difficulty maintaining an erection and his wife was always anorgasmic.

After two years of marriage the couple separated briefly when the wife discovered that the patient had developed a close relationship with a female colleague. However, they returned to each other after two weeks, and sexual intercourse resumed the former pattern. After the first child was born, the wife felt even less support from her husband, resulting in more rows and arguments. When a second child was born the couple were barely on speaking terms. When they were referred for treatment the wife's chief complaint was that her husband was never at home. His main complaint was that when he was at home she nagged him. He sometimes went to public houses with his colleagues which his wife objected to because they never went anywhere together.

From this history two main problems were isolated:

(1) Gross marital disharmony resulting from total lack of satisfactory sexual intercourse, inability to share household responsibilities and lack of communication about everyday matters.
(2) Inability to engage in group discussion with unknown people due to feeling an 'outsider' causing avoidance of social situations.

Treatment of the first problem was by contract marital therapy, and the actual contract drawn up was:

husband's contract
1. To read bedtime stories on 3 nights weekly to the children.
2. To polish children's shoes on 3 days per week.
3. To inform wife what time he will return home from work. If delayed, to telephone 30 minutes before pre-arranged arrival time.

wife's contract
1. To do washing up 3 nights weekly and make husband a cup of tea each night.
2. To set table for breakfast 3 days per week.
3. To have bath prepared for husband on his return from work.

The **first session** was spent establishing the history and target problems, and in the **second session** the above marital contract was worked out. By the **third session** the couple reported back on the contract and apart from one evening when the husband 'forgot' his third task, all was going well and they had each kept to the agreed arrangement of interchanging positive behaviour as laid out in the contract.

In the **fourth session** sexual skills re-education was the focus. They viewed a film on 'tenderness' and instructions were given for non-genital sensate focus practice. They began by massaging each others hands and were instructed to tell each other how this felt. They began to enjoy kissing and cuddling. At this stage the therapist told them *not* to proceed to intercourse and the importance of this was emphasised. They were each instructed in self-masturbation first alone, then in each other's presence. The wife had never before masturbated, and recounted how she had felt a considerable achievement in being able to explore her own body for the first time. They were then given instructions in how to practice the "squeeze" technique (as described by Masters and Johnson).

By **session 6** they were confident enough to proceed to full sexual intercourse, and they reported this was successful when the squeeze technique was used. Both were pleased about the success in this area, despite the fact that the wife was unsure about whether she was experiencing true orgasm. With the use of contracts at the same time the marital situation had improved and they were now having an enjoyable social life.

Session 8 switched to focus onto the husband's social difficulty and he was given practice playing 'host' at a dinner party in a "role play" situation. This was so effective in one session that it was arranged to practise this in real life: the couple invited another couple to dinner, with the husband practising his new role as host. They were also encouraged towards shared social activities such as going to the theatre and cinema. By **session 10** they could be discharged as the marital and sexual situation was now satisfying to both: they described the therapy themselves as "learning to fall in love again."

At the end of the treatment the husband still had some social anxieties at work, but he did not find these a major handicap in his life. He was now able to speak in staff meetings and coped much better with authority figures. In addition he had no difficulties in the sexual sphere: he could maintain an erection and was not troubled by premature ejaculation as before. His wife was orgasmic during coitus on two out of three occasions. Both were delighted with their sexual relationship and found it very satisfying. Unlike before, they engaged in prolonged foreplay and mutual masturbation. They continued to increase their circle of friends by inviting other couples for dinner parties. On these occasions the husband was able to exercise his new-found skills. At the same time, he gave pleasure to his wife and expanded the quality of their relationship leading to an increase in affection on both sides.

Sometimes, sexual problems are the basis of marital discord in which case they should be the main focus of therapy. The pioneering work of Masters and Johnson (1970) is of major importance in this area, and although Masters and Johnson do not call themselves behaviour therapists, their approach clearly fits into this model. One of the many useful techniques they describe is called "sensate focus" which involves exploration of each partner's body by the other, to discover the most pleasurable ways of touching each other. It is important that the 'passive' partner provides constant feedback by telling the 'active' partner which actions he/she finds most pleasurable. The use of this technique to treat a case of non-consumation is illustrated below.

The patient was a forty year old woman whose main problem consisted of non-consumation of marriage of ten years duration and also moderately severe agoraphobia of fifteen years duration. The non-consumation was caused by both premature ejaculation of the husband and vaginismus in the wife. After marriage they frequently attempted intercourse but after five years annulled the marriage on the grounds of non-consumation, although they continued living together. The sexual relationship immediately prior to assessment was restricted to mutual masturbation to orgasm in both partners, and the motivation for seeking treatment was a desire to conceive a child before the wife became too old.

The first part of the **treatment** was devoted to conjoint interviews concerning the sexual problem, after which the couple said they felt closer, and mutual masturbation increased prior to the second interview. The couple and therapist now discussed sexual techniques to be used in a training programme including the 'give-to-get' principle, and sensate focus. Homework was set consisting of mutual caressing over three days, first excluding and then including the genitals. Attempts at sexual intercourse were banned. At the third treatment session two weeks later, both partners reported increased sexual arousal and less anxiety during sensate focus. The patient had exceeded instructions in allowing her husband to insert the tip of one finger into her vagina. The couple were instructed to continue with sensate focus but now with increased exploration of the wife's vagina first by her own and then by her husband's finger. Then they were also asked to buy a lubricant and intercourse was still banned. By the fifth conjoint interview penile penetration of the vagina had taken place with continuing sensate focus and intermittent digital dilation of the vagina. The use of a vaginal lubricant made these prescribed exercises easier and more pleasurable, allowing deeper penetration of the vagina and intravaginal ejaculation. Duration of intercourse was increased by a home programme of sensate focus, extended foreplay and minimal movement during intromission. Penetration, intromission and sexual arousal continued to improve.

The "sensate focus" technique can be used for other kinds of sexual dysfunction where it provides an introduction to increasing intimacy after which specific techniques such as the penile squeeze technique may be introduced, if the main problem is premature ejaculation in the male. Here the woman stimulates the penis to a point just short of ejaculation and the man informs her when this point is reached. When he signals this, she squeezes the frenulum of the penis tightly between thumb and forefingers. This has the effect of inhibiting ejaculation and after practice, ejaculation can be delayed in this way for increasing lengths of time. Other specific techniques will not be described here as details are given fully in Masters and Johnson (1970).

There are now a large number of outcome studies of behavioural marital therapy. The best reviews of such studies are by Olson (1970), Wells, Dilkes and Trivelli (1972) and Gurman (1973). In a recent controlled study, Azrin, Naster and Jones (1973) carried out marital contract therapy along the lines of Stuart on twelve couples. In contrast to "catharsis counselling" the behavioural procedure produced more change. Liberman et al. (1975) found that couple group therapy was more effective in certain ways if the couples had specific training in communication, than if they had the more traditional group therapy. Crowe (1976) has reported the most recent study of marital therapy with 42 couples, in which a directive technique (based on Stuart and some of Masters and Johnson techniques) was contrasted with an interpretative approach (based on that of Skynner (1969) and some of the system theory techniques) and a control procedure involving non-directive intervention. All three techniques were given for an equivalent amount of time, and the results showed them all to be effective for improving marital adjustment, and there were no significant differences between them or that measure. But in measures of sexual adjustment, "target symptoms" and general adjustment the order of effectiveness was (1) directive, (2) interpretative and (3) supportive, with significant differences between directive and supportive approaches. This superiority of the directive behavioural approach was maintained at 18 months follow-up. There is thus a consensus in the field of marital therapy that directive behavioural approaches seem to produce better improvement than supportive measures.

Summary

(1) The only way couples will understand each other is to take notice of what the other person says and does.

(2) Each partner must take the responsibility for initiating the changes they want and not wait for the other person to act first.

(3) The 'give-to-get' principle should be used: this is where each partner rewards the other for carrying out behaviour they like in him or her.

(4) *Positive* behaviours however trivial should be looked for, e.g. "decorating a room" rather than "not paying me attention."

(5) *Specific* detailed behaviour should be elaborated to form the basis of "contracts", e.g. do not accept general requests like "be more affectionate."

(6) As the desired behaviours increase new targets are set for joint discussion with the couple in subsequent sessions.

(7) For sexual problems the procedure is to find out what each partner wants, what part of the process of intercourse is most satisfactory, and to give it on an exchange or *'quid pro quo'* basis.

(8) For specific sexual problems (e.g. impotence, premature or delayed ejaculation, vaginismus, lack of orgasm) use Masters and Johnson's approach: non-demanding pleasurable stimulation of each other, combined with specific techniques.

8
Behavioural Principles in Prevention of Neuroses

In medicine the goal of prevention of disease has been acclaimed for many of the scourges of mankind. Smallpox, tuberculosis and diphtheria are mainly diseases of the past and their prevention rested on identification of the cause and immunisation against this. However, in the management of many diseases prevention has failed, and the emphasis is on *care* rather than *cure*: this includes the chronic conditions of the elderly such as arthritis, and the management of patients after acute illness such as myocardial infarction. The eradication of diseases by immunisation can be called **primary** prevention and is clearly an ideal goal. Management by care rather than cure is less ideal but nonetheless prevents a great deal of suffering: this is **secondary** prevention. In addition, there is **tertiary** prevention which involves the prevention of handicaps due to the main disease: the prevention of the bad effects of prolonged bed rest after myocardial infarction is an example of this.

As we are uncertain of the causation of neurosis, primary prevention seems impossible. If neuroses could be prevented and a scientifically-shaped Utopia produced along the lines of Skinner's novel "Walden Two," would this be a good idea? Possibly neurosis has a survival value to the culture and if totally suppressed or prevented society would not necessarily become happier. We can, however, make a few specific suggestions about primary prevention of phobic neuroses. One of these derives from the folk lore notion that if a person has experienced great fear in a specific situation he should face up to that situation again as soon as possible, e.g. on falling from a horse the rider should remount as soon as possible after the accident, as the longer he waits the more difficult it will become. Aircraft pilots know that this principle applies, and after a recent serious accident of a well-known air display team, the pilots took off again immediately, to prevent a flying phobia developing. Child rearing practices could incorporate this knowledge, although a study of phobic children suggested that the life span of most phobias in children appears to be between 2 weeks and 2 years, with most phobias dissipating within one year of onset (Hampe *et al.*, 1973). On common sense grounds it would seem important that children are not exposed to parents who "model" phobic or obsessional behaviour. Treatment of the adult population may reduce the chances of obsessional or phobic illness developing in their children if modelling plays a part in the aetiology of these conditions. Primary prevention might also become feasible if those populations at psychological risk could be detected. Some research is underway with the aim of developing instruments for the large-scale screening of those members of the population who are susceptible to neurosis but still manage to function adequately (Poser, 1976). In the first step of this project psychological screening tests have been given to groups of high school students in Canada. Approximately 15% of the 10th graders tested appeared "at risk" on the criteria used. A two year follow-up is planned to evaluate the effect of preventative measures that were applied to this group.

Secondary prevention, or care rather than cure, has been what the majority of this book has been about. However, this chapter offers a preventive treatment of anxiety states in this sense: the treatment aims to prevent *future* attacks of anxiety by teaching the patient a self-coping technique. Suinn and Richardson (1972) proposed an "anxiety management training" programme to teach coping skills to test-anxious subjects. Meichenbaum (1971) has devised techniques of teaching coping skills to anxious people which he calls "stress innoculation" training. This latter term is best avoided as, because of its medical associations, it implies primary prevention for a technique of secondary prevention. A technique that draws on work by Suinn *et al.* (1972) and Meichenbaum *et al.* (1974) is best illustrated by an example.

Anxiety Management Training

Bill came to me via the 24 hour emergency service of the Maudsley Hospital. He said that he kept having attacks of severe anxiety in which he felt he was going to die. This had been going on for three years and no special event brought them on. During the attack he felt his heart beating fast, his hair standing on end, he sweated profusely and had to rush off for reassurance, usually to a hospital. He had had five such attacks in the last month and found tranquillisers were not helpful.

Treatment began by giving him a rationale for his anxiety. He was told that the early symptoms of anxiety which were harmless in themselves served to make him more anxious and this in turn gave him more severe symptoms. In other words, the anxiety was explained to him in Schacterian terms, i.e. the patient feels anxious *because* he experiences increased heart rate, sweating palms, rapid breathing, etc. The Schacter and Singer theory of emotions is not widely accepted by psychologists, but happens to be a useful way of conceptualising anxiety for patients. Alternative explanations may be given.

Then he was asked to settle back in a comfortable arm chair and rehearse saying things to himself which emphasised his ability to cope with his own anxiety.

The actual coping self-statements he practised were:

(1) "Don't think about fear, just think about relaxing in an armchair."
(2) "This anxiety is just what the doctor said I'd feel."
(3) "This is not the worst thing that can happen."
(4) "I can handle the situation if I don't think about dying."
(5) "I can cope with this anxiety without rushing off to hospital."
(6) "The doctor explained I would not die and I know that really."

After his anxiety was reduced in this way, he followed this with:

(7) "I really coped with that on my own."
(8) "I'm getting better each time I practise."
(9) "I didn't need to go to the walk-in clinic that time."
(10) "My doctor will be pleased with this progress."

To begin with, the patient and therapist repeated statements 1–6 *out loud.* Then the patient *alone* repeated statements 1–6. Next he *whispered* the same statements as before and finally repeated each of them to himself (i.e. subvocally). When he had achieved this, the reinforcing self-statements 7–10 were used similarly.

After this procedure had been learnt in the clinic, the patient was told to practise it for one hour each day, and to use it in the real life situation if he actually experienced a panic attack. After four hour-long practice sessions at weekly intervals, he was able to use anxiety management training on his own, and stopped attending the walk-in clinic without appointments.

This short-term successful result of preventing attendances at an emergency clinic in a single case does not of course prove the usefulness of the method, and controlled studies are awaited. Even in this case we do not yet know the long term result. However, Meichenbaum has demonstrated that it is more helpful to practise *coping* statements rather than statements concerned with overcoming or mastering the situation (Meichenbaum, 1973). Part of the problem of psychological treatment approaches to anxiety states in a psychiatric population is that anxiety management training requires a great deal of cooperation on the part of the patient. He must attend regularly and be prepared to work hard at treatment. Also specially trained therapists must be available for these techniques. It would certainly be easier were an effective medication available for anxiety states. The patient described had tried using alcohol himself to relieve anxiety, but this had only transient effects, as did diazepam prescribed by his general practitioner.

Where anxiety is experienced by a patient such as Bill, the anxiety is not attached to a situation or object, this is called "free-floating anxiety." As no situation or object precipitates the attack the only treatment approach possible is prevention, and here Schachter's cognitive model of anxiety, which states that anxiety begins *after* the appraisal of danger, may be helpful (Schachter, 1966).

Anxiety can begin with physiological changes which are then followed by subjective sensations of anxiety, e.g. anxiety can *follow* the tensing of skeletal musculature as well as cause it. A feedback loop may be involved whereby heightened emotion produces physiological changes (the patient says to himself "I'm aware of my heart beating." This awareness makes the patient feel "my heart is beating fast and I might die" which further exacerbates anxiety and reinforces itself and the patient thinks to himself "now I feel much worse which confirms the idea that I'm going to die." *Clinical Anxiety* differs from normal anxiety in being more severe, more persistent, and inappropriate to the patient's situation at the same time.

Anxiety states or free-floating anxiety are characterised by symptoms produced by over-activity of the sympathetic and parasympathetic nervous system. The main symptoms are palpitations, apprehension, respiratory distress, dizziness, sweating, fainting, diarrhoea, irritability, tremor, pain in the chest, poor concentration and feelings of impending death and disaster. In between attacks the patient loses these symptoms, but often does not feel completely well.

There is no doubt that anxiety states are common. They accounted for 27% of patients who saw their General Practitioners in a London practice (Kedward and Cooper, 1966) and 8% of all outpatients attending the Maudsley Hospital Outpatients. Kedward and Cooper's study of General Practice found that 74% of the anxious patients were female but other studies in a psychiatric practice showed the sexes to be equally represented. Anxiety states occur in young adult life, and genetic studies show that there is often a constitutional tendency.

The helplessness concept

Whether or not an anxiety state develops in any one individual may depend on the amount of stress to which he is subjected. On the other hand, anxiety or depression may be caused by what Seligman (1975) has called "uncontrollable reward." He described an experiment in which groups of hungry rats had pellets of food dropped 'from the sky' through a hole in the roof of their cage independently of their responses; then they had to learn to get food by pressing a bar. The rats who received 'free' food did worse at learning instrumental responses for food: "Some of the rats just sat around for days, waiting for more food to drop in; they never pressed the bar."

In a related study entitled "The Pigeon in a Welfare State" one group of hungry pigeons learned to jump on a pedal for grain. A 'welfare state' group received the same grain regardless of its responses, and a third group received no grain. All groups were then taught to obtain grain by pecking a lighted key. The group that had controlled grain by pedal pressing learnt to obtain grain faster, the control group next, and the 'welfare state' group slowest. The results are controversial, but along with other evidence provided by Seligman of the debilitating effects of uncontrollable reward they may provide some clues to the prevention of neurosis. The helplessness theory predicts that when uncontrollable events occur depression will be predisposed, and to the degree that controllable events occur, a sense of mastery and resistance to depression will result.

Ideally all therapy should be preventive: it should equip the patient with a repertoire of coping responses which he could use at all times when he found his usual phobic, obsessional or depressive responses ineffective. However, behavioural techniques at the present time are more effective in teaching coping procedure that *care* for the patient rather than *cure* him. We should not feel too pessimistic about this state of affairs, however, as considerable progress has been made since Thomas Browne stated in 1680: 'We all labour against our own cure; for death is the cure of all diseases.'

‖ References and Bibliography

Ayllon, T. and Azrin, N. H. (1968) "The Token Economy" Appleton-Century-Crofts, New York.

Azrin, N. H. and Nunn, R. G. (1974) A rapid method of eliminating stuttering by a regulated breathing approach. *Behaviour Research and Therapy* **12,** 279–286.

Azrin, N. H., Naster, B. J. and Jones, R. (1973) Reciprocity Counselling: a rapid learning-based procedure for marital counselling. *Behaviour Research and Therapy* **11,** 365–382.

Bancroft, J. (1970) A comparative study of aversion and desensitization in the treatment of homosexuality. *In* "Behaviour Therapy in the 1970's" L. E. Burns and J. L. Worsley (Eds) J. Wright, Bristol.

Bandura, A. (1970) Psychotherapy based upon modeling principles. *In* "Handbook of Psychotherapy" A. E. Bergin and S. L. Garfield (Eds) Wiley, New York.

Benjamin, S., Marks, I. M. and Huson, J. (1972) Active muscular relaxation in desensitization of phobic patients. *Psychological Medicine* **2,** 381–390.

Brady, J. P. (1971) Metronome-conditioned speech retraining for stuttering. *Behavior Therapy* **2,** 129–150.

Bringmann, W. G., Kricher, A. and Balance, W. (1970) Goethe as behaviour therapist. *Journal of the History of Behaviour Sciences* **25,** 151–155.

Browne, Sir Thomas (1680) *Religio Medici*, II, 9.

Burgess, A. (1972) "A Clockwork Orange" Penguin Books, London.

Cautela, J. R. (1966) Treatment of behaviour by covert sensitization. *Psychological Record* **16,** 33–41

Crowe, M. J. (1976) Behaviour Treatments in Psychiatry. *In* "Recent Advances in Clinical Psychiatry" K. Granville-Grossman (Ed.) Churchill-Livingstone, Edinburgh.

Cullen, W. (1971) *In* "History of the Term 'Neurosis'" Knoppff, W. F. (Ed.) Paper to Vth World Congress of Psychiatry, Mexico.

Falloon, I. and Gough, A. (1975) Behaviour therapy: the role of the occupational therapist. *Occupational Therapy* 145–146.

Falloon, I., Lindley, P. and McDonald, B. (1974) A Social Training Manual. Unpublished manuscript.

Feldman, M. P. (1973) Abnormal sexual behaviour in males. *In* "Handbook of Abnormal Psychology" (2nd edn) H. J. Eysenck (Ed.) Pitman, London.

Foreyt, J. P. and Kennedy, W. A. (1971) Treatment of overweight by aversion therapy. *Behaviour Research and Therapy* **9,** 29–34.

Fransella, F. (1976) Stuttering: some facts and treatments. *British Journal of Hospital Medicine* 70–78.

Friedman, D. E. and Lipsedge, M. S. (1971) Treatment of phobic anxiety and psychogenic impotence by systematic desensitization employing methohexitone-induced relaxation. *British Journal of Psychiatry* **118,** 87–90.

Gelder, M. G., Marks, I. M. and Wolff, H. H. (1967) Desensitization and psychotherapy in the treatment of phobic states: A controlled enquiry. *British Journal of Psychiatry* **113,** 53–73.

General Register Office (1968) A Glossary of Mental Disorders. Based on International Statistical Classification of Diseases, Injuries and Causes of Death (1965, 8th Revision), H.M.S.O.

Gurman, A. (1973) The effects and effectiveness of marital therapy: a review of outcome research. *Family Process* **12,** 145.

Hampe, E., Noble, H., Miller, L. C. and Barrett, C. L. (1973) Phobic children one and two years post treatment. *Journal of Abnormal Psychology* **82,** 446–453.

Hegeler, I. and Hegeler, S. (1963) "An ABZ of Love" Spearman, Great Britain.

Jacobsen, E. "Progressive Relaxation" University of Chicago Press, Chicago, 1938.

Johnson, D., Lancashire, M., Mathews, A. M., Munby, M., Shaw, P. M. and Gelder, M. G. (1976) Imaginal flooding and exposure to real phobic situations: changes during treatment. *British Journal of Psychiatry* **129,** 372.

Kanfer, F. H. (1976) 8th International Banff Conference.

Kanfer, F. H. and Phillips, J. S. (1970) "Learning Foundations of Behaviour Therapy" Wiley, New York.

Kedward, H. B. and Cooper, B. (1966) Neurotic disorders in urban practice: a 3-year follow up. *Journal of College of General Practitioners* **12,** 148–163.

Kumar, K. and Wilkinson, J. C. M. (1971) Thought stopping: a useful treatment in phobias of 'internal stimuli'. *British Journal of Psychiatry* **119,** 305–307.

Lewis, A. J. (1936) Problems of obsessional illness. *Proceedings of Royal Society of Medicine* **29,** 325–336.

Lewis, A. J. (1957) Obsessional illness. *Acta Neuropsiquiatrica argent.* 323–335.

Liberman, R. P. (1970) Behavioural approaches in family and couple therapy. *American Journal of Orthopsychiatry* **40,** 106.

Liberman, R. P., Levine, J., Wheeler, E., Sanders, N. and Wallace, C. (1975) Experimental evaluation of marital group therapy: behavioural vs. interaction – insight formats. Program Report, Camarillo Research Centre, Camarillo, California, U.S.A.

Maletzky, B. M. (1973) "Assisted" covert sensitization: a preliminary report. *Behavior Therapy* **4,** 117–119.

Marks. I. M. (1969) "Fears and Phobias" Heinemann Medical, London.

Marks, I. M. (1975) Behavioural treatments of phobic and obsessive-compulsive disorders: a critical appraisal. *In* "Progress in Behaviour Therapy" Hersen, R. *et al.* (Eds) Academic Press, New York, London.

Marks, I. M. (1978) Behavioural psychotherapy of neurotic disorders. *In* "Handbook of Psycotherapy and Behavior Modifications" (2nd Edn) Garfield, S. and Bergin, A. E. (Eds) John Wiley, New York.

Marks, I. M. and Gelder, M. G. (1966) Common ground between behaviour therapy and psychodynamic methods. *British Journal of Medical Psychology* **39,** 11.

Masters, W. H. and Johnson, V. E. (1970) "Human Sexual Inadequacy" Churchill, London.

McFall, R. M. and Twentyman, C. T. (1973) Four experiments in the relative contributions of rehearsal, modelling and coaching to assertion training. *Journal of Abnormal Psychology* **81,** 199–218.

Meichenbaum, D. H. (1971a) Cognitive factors in behaviour modification: Modifying what clients say to themselves. Paper presented at the meeting of the Association for Advancement of Behavior Therapy, Washington, D.C. September 1971.

Meichenbaum, D. H. (1971b) Examination of model characteristics in reducing avoidance behavior. *Journal of Personality and Social Psychology* **17,** 298–307.

Meichenbaum, D. H. (1972) Cognitive modification of test anxious college students. *Journal of Consulting and Clinical Psychology* **39,** 370–380.

Meichenbaum, D. H. and Cameron, R. (1974) An examination of cognitive and contingency variables in anxiety relief procedures. Unpublished manuscript.

Meichenbaum, D. H., Gilmore, J. B. and Fedoravicius, A. (1971) Group insight versus group desensitization in treatment of speech anxiety. *Journal of Consulting and Clinical Psychology* **36,** 410–421.

Olson, D. H. (1970) Marital and Family Therapy: Integrative Review and Critique. *Journal of Marriage and the Family* **32,** 501–538.

Poser, E. (1976) Strategies for prevention of neurosis. Paper to 6th European Association for Behaviour Therapy, Greece.

Rachman, S. (1966) Studies in desensitization: II. Flooding. *Behaviour Research and Therapy* **4,** 1–15.

Rachman, S. (1969) Treatment by prolonged exposure to high intensity stimulation. *Behaviour Research and Therapy* **7,** 295–302.

Rachman, S. (1971) Obsessional ruminations. *Behaviour Research and Therapy*

9, 229–235.

Rachman, S. (1972) Clinical application of observational learning, imitation, and modeling. *Behavior Therapy* **3,** 379–397.

Rachman, S. (1974) Primary obsessional slowness. *Behaviour Research and Therapy* **12,** 9–18.

Rachman, S. and Teasdale, J. (1969) "Aversion Therapy and Behaviour Disorders" Routledge and Kegan Paul, London.

Rachman, S., Marks, I. M. and Hodgson, R. (1971) The treatment of obsessive-compulsive neuroses. *Behaviour Research and Therapy* **9,** 237–247.

Rachman, S., Marks, I. M. and Hodgson, R. (1973) The treatment of obsessive-compulsive neurotics by modeling and flooding in vivo. *Behaviour Research and Therapy* **11,** 463–471.

Roper, G. and Rachman, S. (1976) Obsessional-compulsive checking: experimental replication and development. *Behaviour Research and Therapy* **14,** 25–32.

Schachter, S. (1966) *In* "Anxiety and Behaviour" C. D. Spielberger (Ed.) Academic Press, New York, London.

Seligman, M. E. P. (1975) "Helplessness: On Depression, Development and Death" W. H. Freeman and Company, San Francisco.

Skinner, B. F. (1948) "Walden Two" Macmillan, New York.

Skynner, A. C. R. (1969) A group analytic approach to conjoint family therapy. *Journal of Child Psychology and Psychiatry* **10,** 81.

Stampfl, T. G. and Levis, D. G. (1967) Essentials of implosive therapy: a learning theory based psychodynamic behaviour therapy. *Journal of Abnormal Psychology* **72,** 496–503.

Stampfl, T. G. (1967) *In* "Behavior Modification Techniques in the Treatment of Emotional Disorders" S. G. Armitage (Ed.) Battle Creek, Mich.: V.A. Publication, Pp. 22–37.

Stern, R. S. (1970) Treatment of a case of obsessional neurosis using thought stopping technique. *British Journal of Psychiatry* **117,** 441–442.

Stern, R. S. and Marks, I. M. (1973) Brief and prolonged flooding: A comparison in agoraphobic patients. *Archives of General Psychiatry* **28,** 270–276.

Stern, R. S., Lipsedge, M. S. and Marks, I. M. (1973) Thought-stopping of neutral and obsessive thoughts: a controlled trial. *Behaviour Research and Therapy* **11,** 659–662.

Stuart, R. B. (1969) Operant-interpersonal treatment for marital discord. *Journal of Consulting and Clinical Psychology* **33,** 675.

Suinn, R. M. and Richardson, F. (1971) Anxiety management training: A non-specific behavior therapy program for anxiety control. *Behavior Therapy* **2,** 498–510.

Wallerstein, R. S. (1957) "Hospital Treatment of Alcoholism: A Comparative Experimental Study" Basic Books, New York.

Waters, W. F., McDonald, D. G. and Koresko, R. L. (1972) Psychophysiological responses during analogue desensitization and non-relaxation control procedures. *Behaviour Research and Therapy* **10,** 381–393.

Wells, R. A., Dilkes, T. C. and Trivelli, N. (1972) The results of family therapy: a critical review of the literature. *Family Process* **11,** 189.

Wilson, G. T. and Davidson, G. C. (1969) Aversion techniques in behaviour therapy: Some theoretical and metatheoretical considerations. *Journal of Consulting and Clinical Psychology* **33,** 327–329.

Wolpe, J. (1958) "Psychotherapy by Reciprocal Inhibition" Stanford University Press, Stanford.

Wolpe, J. (1969) "The Practice of Behaviour Therapy" Pergamon Press, New York.

Wolpe, J. and Lazarus, A. A. (1966) "Behaviour Therapy Techniques" Pergamon Press, New York.

Yamagami, T. (1971) The treatment of an obsession by thought-stopping. *Journal of Behaviour Therapy and Experimental Psychiatry* **2,** 233–239.

‖ Suggested Additional Reading List

Books on behaviour therapy or related subjects which the reader may find a useful supplement:

BANDURA, A. "Principles of Behaviour Modification." New York; Holt, Rinehart & Winston (1969).

BEECH, H. R. "Obsessional States." Methuen (1974).

FRANKS, C. M. and WILSON, G. T. "Annual Review of Behaviour Therapy, Theory, & Practice." Vol. 1: 1973, Vol. 2: 1974, Vol. 3: 1975, etc. Brunner/Mazel, New York.

LADER, M. and MARKS, I. "Clinical Anxiety." Heinemann (1971).

MARKS, I. M. "Fears and Phobias." Heinemann (1969).

MEYER, V. and CHESSER, E. S. "Behaviour Therapy in Clinical Psychiatry." Penguin Books (1970).

SELIGMAN, M. E. P. "Helplessness: on Depression, Development & Death." Freeman (1975).

Journals devoted to behaviour therapy:

Behaviour Research & Therapy

Behavior Therapy: Journal of the Association for Advancement of Behavior Therapy

Journal of Behavior Therapy & Experimental Psychiatry

‖ Index